The Joy of Surrender unto Him!

First published 2004
Revised and reprinted 2014

Solace Community
PO Box 416
Sevenoaks
Kent, England
TN14 6WE
office@mothersprayers.org
www.mothersprayers.org

ISBN 0 9547321 5 4

Published in Great Britain by
Transform Management Ltd
E mail: info@1025transform.co.uk

ACKNOWLEDGEMENTS

My grateful thanks to John Edwards S.J. for his invaluable advice and direction, and to Family Publications for permission to use an extract from Fr Edwards' book "Ways of Loving" reproduced on pages 102–104.

Also to members of our community for their help in proof reading this book.

My grateful thanks also to Norbert Jung for the wonderful cover design; norbert@esprit-photo.com

All proceeds from this book will be donated to the work of the Solace Community, registered Charity 1061402/0.

Pictured on the front cover is Caroline (French Coordinator of Mothers Prayers) and on the back cover from left to right; Caroline, Veronica and Ruth of the Solace Community.

INTRODUCTION

So many of us have been conditioned to think that 'God helps those who help themselves.' But I am convinced that God helps us even more, when we decide to allow Him to reign fully in us.

He has given us a Free Will and so it is up to us just how much we invite Him into our lives!

This little book is about surrender, but the very word 'surrender' for some reason seems to frighten many people and often their first thought is 'what will I have to give up?' and then 'does it mean that I will lose control over all the situations in my life?'

However I have found a wonderful joy through the 'surrender' of my life into the Will of God, Our Father, and experienced His amazing and loving guidance in so many ways!

So I have written this book to help calm any fears that anyone may have and I hope that in sharing my experiences, the reader will come to understand 'surrender' in a real way and so be encouraged to find the same joy in their life too.

Veronica

Introduction – by Benedict M. Heron OSB

"The Joy of Surrender unto Him" by Veronica Williams. This is a book which deserves to be very widely read, and I am confident that it will be. I think that many people will be spiritually helped by reading it, as indeed I have been myself.

We live in times when, at least in our part of the world, many Christian movements are drooping if not dying. Less people are going to church on Sundays, less people coming forward for the priesthood or ministry, churches being closed, the younger generation being noticeable by their absence in church services, financial difficulties, the breakdown of Christian marriage, widespread unbelief.

At the same time there are some Christian movements and church centres which are very flourishing, indeed sometimes exploding.

Mothers Prayers is one of these. To have gone from nothing to being in more than eighty countries in eight years, and this without any publicity drives, is humanly speaking quite impossible.

How did it happen, is it happening? It can only be explained, in my opinion, as a special outpouring of the Holy Spirit. In this book Veronica Williams writes with wisdom and insight on the spirituality behind the movement, which stresses much the importance of surrendering everything to God, and the joy which this brings. When the Mothers Prayers groups meet together they surrender to God, to Jesus, each of their children. Then they worship and praise. It is all very simple, but it is also the key to Christian living. Along side this profound teaching we have the account of how much of this happened. Endless trusting in God and prayer and praise surrendering everything to Him, listening to God to see what He is doing and co-operating with that.

All this leading to numerous co-incidences which one can only describe as God - incidences. Behind all this there is the Bible and great appreciation of the Eucharist.

This book and the story behind it is what I call a 'spiritual thriller' It will, I am confident, strengthen your faith and the faith of many other people.

FOREWORD

Reassuringly, much of what Veronica Williams says about "Surrender" has classic parallels. De Caussade speaks of Abandonment to Divine Providence, Brother Lawrence of the Practice of the Presence of God.

It seems one can identify what she speaks of in their words. And with her too there are arresting consequences from the Act of Surrender, in the way of finding God's Will.

Of course surrender costs. It may involve giving up possessions, and you must not care if you are rich or poor (67,72).

I particularly relish the painlessness of breaking crockery (when your own, all the bits you loved, is no longer your possession) (59).

It can be a challenge (82).

A basic prayer life is essential: private prayer, prayer in a group, Bible reading,

And daily Mass (if possible).

But fundamental is conviction of God's love of us: with that, there is bound to be Joy.

And it works. To be relaxed in crisis; at peace before talks which do not need preparation (45,46); free from fear and worry – about the future, about change, about decisions, about what people think (93). All this is no small proof. Above all the extraordinary worldwide spread of Mothers Prayers is the overwhelming example of God's lavish generosity to one who has 'surrendered'. And, again and always, Joy.

Prayer of course is basic. God gives pictures and thoughts and words in prayer (15,17,22,25,31) pictures or words on waking (17,25). She does nothing but pray when she has received certainty, until God wants the next step.(19,22,37,41,49,58). It's a prayer not only at set times, but at all times and all places: she is one who finds God in all things, who is a contemplative in action.

Examples of prudent procedures. She always prays about a projected situation (21,26,34). She expects God to give certainty when the right decision is made (23).

She implements His Will, when it is known, by ordinary human mechanisms (22). And this former successful business woman is eminently practical and down to earth.

She never initiates (22); she is only God's secretary (37,44), she finds God facilitates and implements (22,49,58 and passim). And it is He who brings people to help (22,25,28,36) and gives openings (39,41,49,61).

But if this sounds enthusiastic and unorthodox, note that she is subservient to "the Church" and accepts suggestions from companions (22).

And every detail of a showing has to be verified if she is to proceed.

It is not so much that she seeks confirmation in surprising ways but that when these occur the Holy Spirit seems to kick in with consolation – which she registers.

Veronica is safe and orthodox. Just rather remarkable. Read the book.

John Edwards S.J.

SECTION 1. Reasons for Surrender:

1. What Surrender is

2. Happiness & Joy

3. Full potential

4. Love of God

SECTION 2. A consequence of Surrender: finding God's Will:

Instances:

1 Illumination through prayer

2 Easter Festival

3 Mothers Prayers

4 Moving Office

5 Pentecost Celebration

6 Medical

7 Other peoples' Experience

8 General

Other consequences.

SECTION 3. How to Surrender, and how God's guidance comes:

1 Love God

2 Know God

3 Practical steps

SECTION 4. Scripture and Prayer.

Section 1: Reasons for Surrender

1. What Surrender is:

I have, for a number of years, loved to talk about 'surrender'.

I am sure that already those of you who know me well, will be nodding your head in agreement as you read these words,

I remember that at one of the conferences for Mothers Prayers, a friend of mine who is an Anglican vicar, and had agreed to give the homily, started his talk with the words… 'Hands up any one who *hasn't* heard Veronica talk about surrender'

His words were greeted with laughter!

Everyone there knew that the topic of surrender is very dear to my heart.

But let me explain, that when I speak of surrender – I am speaking of 100% surrender!

Now, are you among those people who might feel concerned by this thought?

If so, you are not alone! In fact when I have discussed this topic in the past, I have noticed that the reaction of the majority of people is usually; 'Oh I'm not sure'

There seems to be no problem at all with 75% surrender (or 80%, even 95%) but 100%?

If you feel concerned, I would guess the reason might be that you feel in the future you will not have control over the way you wish to live your life.

You may also wonder what would be taken away from you, or what you would have to give up.

There is usually a small area in all of our lives that we feel we want to hold on to.

(Once we have the courage to let go of this, we often wonder why it was so important to us and why it took so long.)

Sometimes we find that this was the very thing that had been blocking our happiness.

However, another reaction has been 'I would like to know more about surrender'.

So I have been asked if I would share with you my own experiences in the hope that it will be an encouragement and help for you to see the beauty of surrender.

It does seem to me that because it is, basically, such a simple thing to do, people often overlook it in favour of seeking more complicated ways to become 'holy'.

First of all I feel it may be helpful to think in terms of 'allowing' instead of *'surrender'* because for me, 100% surrender has simply meant giving God full permission to *allow* Him to be the God of my life.

I understand now that as we 'surrender' and 'allow' Almighty God into our life, we are asking Him to guide us in His ways, and we are giving Him _full_ permission to give us all that is necessary for us to be truly happy and so live life to the full.

In this 'allowing' we also give Him permission to change us into the person He created us to be, and to change any area of our life that needs to be changed so that we may live in peace and joy.

He is such a tender, loving Lord; He waits patiently for us to invite Him more and more into our lives.

2. *Happiness & Joy*

We all want to be happy, don't we? And today there seems to be so many ways in which we are encouraged to seek happiness.

We may look for this in our relationships, or maybe through our work and why not?

Some may think that by moving to a different or larger house or to another area, will make them happy.

And when any new fad comes along, we so often see people rush to try them, hoping that this will be the answer for their unhappiness.

We often hear people say – 'I know I would be really happy if I could lose some weight' (does this sound familiar?)

Others believe that the latest food supplement which promises to give them better health, or a new relaxation method will be the answer, and others through visiting the Gym!

It always amazes me just how much pain people will put themselves through just to get fit.

Often articles in magazines encourage young people to think that they will be much happier by following the latest fashion and by having clothes with the latest designer label.

So, it does seem that many of us live our lives constantly thinking 'I am sure I will be happy when….'

Or maybe some of us are living with regret, thinking 'if only I could have that….'

We do seem to be forever chasing and striving after happiness, and somehow the more we chase the more it seems to elude us!

We may be very unhappy about the situations in our children's lives, and feel if only this or that would change....

Yes, we seem to spend such a lot of time on the 'if only's...' and in trying to sort out what we think will make us happy!

Not everyone is like this I know, and there are many people who seek happiness in really selfless ways and are very blessed by the Lord.

Praise the Lord for the wonderful example they are to us.

But it does seem that *'Happiness'* or the lack of it is usually linked with the circumstances of our lives and is often dependent on other people.

We can feel 'happy' because all seems to be well, the sun is shining, or someone is being kind to us, but then how do we feel when the clouds come, or when our friends turn against us and the bottom seems to fall out of our lives.

'Joy' on the other hand is quite different; it is not subject to any circumstance, but remains with us even during all the problems in our lives.

It comes as a result of our relationship with the Lord; of being in close contact with Him, and knowing that whatever happens He is there to hold us close to Him.

I am sure you will know of someone who has many problems but always seems to be smiling. They are such a wonderful example to us and show the world that by trusting in the love and care of the Lord, it is possible to be at peace, in spite of all the pain around us.

The joy that they experience is a sign of their inner peace and that they have taken to heart the words in 1 Peter 5 v7 'unload all your burden on to Him since He is concerned for you…'.

And this Joy, which so often radiates from them and is a sign of the indwelling of the Holy Spirit, is one of the most powerful means of evangelising others. People who are searching for happiness and looking for the meaning for life will be attracted to this 'JOY'.

I understand this much more now, and that the sure way to be truly 'happy', is to have peace of mind, and so be filled with 'Joy'.

This has started to become a reality in my life as I try now to live my life surrendered to the will of the Lord – the One who loves and is Love,

All other ways in which we try to achieve happiness may have a short term success, but then when things change, we are left feeling even more dissatisfied and with a deep yearning still within us!

If you are seeking happiness remember that Our Lord knows what will make you happy.

He created you with a perfect plan in mind for you, one that no –one else can do as well as you. He loves you and He knows the reason that He made you just as you are.

Yes, the Lord has created you exactly as He wanted you to be and has made you to be happy.

You are Royal – a prince or princess, because you are a beloved son or daughter of the King of Kings. You are a work of art.

Maybe you don't feel like a 'work of art' at the moment. Perhaps there are things in your life that seem to be a blockage to any real peace and happiness.

Maybe at this moment, you feel your life is going nowhere or that it is not going the way you want it.

Perhaps you even feel a failure.

Please don't think like this.

He knows all these things and is anxious to help you to get back on the right track towards happiness.

The Lord loves you passionately – He has a plan for *YOU!*

Give Him a chance – you will not regret it.

3. Full Potential

My own story of surrender

I first became aware of the need to make changes in my life, after I had read a book in which the reader was invited to write their own epitaph – to say how they thought others would remember them after they had died.

To my horror, I realised that they would probably say that I was a good businesswoman. I was really shocked. I had never thought about this before.

But I knew that this was probably how most people would remember me. I was quite upset and I thought, 'I don't want to be remembered like this!'

I continued to read on and then saw that it was suggested that we should write *how* we would like to be remembered. Now this was a different matter.

So I wrote I wanted to be remembered as a good mother and grandmother and that my life would have meant something especially with regard to children.

It was only recently that I realised how much the Lord had honoured this deep desire of my heart, by giving me the ministry of 'Mothers Prayers' (see section 2 chapter 3).

Often women I have met through this ministry (even those older than myself) have said to me that they see me as their mother!

Perhaps it will help you if you were to write down what you think people will say about you and then what you would like them to say. This can be very revealing...

Who am I?

The second understanding of my need to change came during this same rather painful period of my life.

I was very confused at this time and was trying desperately to be happy.

I had to please many awkward people – trying to be *this* for one person and *that* for another; I felt that I was wearing too many masks and this, in some ways, was compromising who I was.

I remember thinking 'I don't know who *I* am any more' and understood that I had somehow changed through the many circumstances of my life.

An image of the bottom of a boat came into my mind, with many barnacles clinging on to it – completely changing its appearance and I am sure it's performance.

'This is just how I feel' I thought – 'through every difficult situation and bad experience in my life it has been as though a barnacle had been stuck on to me making me change my shape! When I was born I was *me* – the way the Lord created me' I felt desperately unhappy and felt that I just wanted to become the *real* me.

Now, it might help you to understand if I explain that I am a person who doesn't like to read the instructions for

---

any new appliance, or gadget. I know there are many who feel the same way.

For example, I once bought a microwave, which could also be used as an ordinary oven. Three years later when I moved from this house, leaving the microwave behind, I realised that I had never once used it as an oven – it had always seemed much easier to use the conventional one, than to bother to read the instructions.

I have always felt the same with regard to my washing machine. It really is only necessary for me to have one with two programmes, as that is all I ever use.

Of course I realise that in order to get the full potential from these appliances, I should follow the maker's instructions.

Perhaps it was through the prayers of my mother that I began to consider all this, during this period of confusion in my life. Because it was like a flash of recognition and I began to understand that if I wanted to reach *my* full potential, i.e. to be the person the Lord created me to be, I too must follow my Maker's instructions.

It became so clear to me and I was so sure of the need to hand everything over to Him (because only then I would be truly happy) that I cried out to Him and my prayer was:

'Lord, you know who I am, why you made me, and why I look this way, and why I live here. Lord, I want to be the person you created me to be, not the person that I have become.'

I told Him

'Lord I do not care what it takes, I do not care if I am rich or poor, married or single, sick or healthy.'

I really meant every word, even about the sickness. I was given the grace to think of people I had heard about, who even though they were on their sick beds, still were in total peace, accepting joyfully the Lord's will.

All I now wanted was to be the 'Veronica' He had created me to be.

I somehow knew that from that day, nothing would matter to me except that I should live in His will. I didn't want to be working only on two programmes!

I felt quite excited and knew that there would be changes in my life.

(Yes, I feel that this exciting understanding did come to me through the prayers of my mother. She had always prayed every day for each of her children.)

How the Lord has blessed me through my surrender!

4. The Love of God.

Maybe you are wondering 'What must I do to surrender and what will it mean to my life?'

Or perhaps you feel the cost may prove to be too high.

I do understand that it may *seem* difficult, as it is contrary to our usual way of thinking. We usually feel *we* must strive to 'be in control' and it is *our* responsibility to find all the solutions to our problems.

And so it may be difficult for you to even consider 'surrender' as something to be sought after.

One of the reasons you may be worried, is that you may think that the Lord will want you to be poor and expect you to give everything away, in the same way He asked the rich young man in the Bible.

But only He knows the special plan He has for you, the one that will make you happy and feel fulfilled

If it is for you to work and be amongst the poor, you will never be truly happy if you try to be in any other place.

His plan for you may be to be amongst the rich and if so that is where you will find happiness.

It is more likely that He will wish you to remain just where you are now and by the way you live, be a witness of His love and protection, to your friends, neighbours and people at work.

It is not about being poor or wealthy; it is about being where the Lord wants you to be – to have no agenda of your own, except to do His Will.

And remember that if we do surrender our lives to Him, this includes our financial situation but it also means He will look after our overdrafts.

We are only the managers of His money. There is great freedom in this.

In the past, I have watched the worried expressions of some people when I have touched on the subject of total surrender.

But after I have had the following conversation with them, their expression has usually changed.

I ask them 'are you married?' and when they reply 'yes', I continue; 'when you were standing at the altar on your wedding day, did you not surrender your life to your spouse?

Did you not say, 'for better for worse, for richer for poorer, in sickness and in health, till death do us part' and isn't this 'surrender'?

Were you not willing to go wherever was necessary to support them and to stay with them forever whatever the circumstances?

In other words you both surrendered your lives to each other.

And you did this I am sure because you loved your spouse, and you knew that you were loved too.'

I do wonder why so many people are worried about making similar promises to their Lord and God – He, who can never let them down, who loves them passionately and wishes only for their good!

You may even be thinking I am not good enough; there is too much sin in my life.

The Lord himself said 'I have come to call not the upright but sinners to repentance.'

He knows our hearts and if we sincerely want to come closer to Him, He will take us by the hand and lead us. He waits longingly for our return to Him.

Section 2: A consequence of Surrender: finding God's Will

1. Illumination through prayer.

I am not sure if you will understand this, but the Lord often seems to speak to my heart through images in my mind, during prayer.

I would like to share with you now, two such pictures. They helped me to understand this total surrender, in a way that is easy to explain.

The first picture was of two river banks with a wide, muddy river running between them. There were many ships travelling up and down on it.

I felt that the two banks represented Earth and Heaven and the river symbolised the path through life. Standing on the edge of the bank, which represented Earth was a figure, which I took to be me. Then she jumped into the river of life and started to thrash away with laboured swimming strokes in an attempt to get to the other side: puffing and grunting with all the effort of trying to avoid all the obstacles. At last she reached the other side and lay panting on the shore just grateful to have made it.

The second picture was with the same setting, the same river banks, river, and the same person standing ready to dive in. Then she turned her back to the river and fell gently backwards into it. A large wave came and as she rested on the wave it took her through all the obstacles and gently placed her onto the other shore.

To me this is what surrender is all about – we can either do it under our own effort, calling from time to time to the Lord for help, or we can simply abandon ourselves to Him and He will come like the big wave and carry us through all the obstacles of life.

This doesn't mean we will be free of problems, but we will be carried through them in peace and joy.

And when we receive the gift of surrender it is then that we often experience real peace for the first time in our lives.

It is the Peace the world cannot give.

2. Easter Festival

To illustrate the way the Lord guides and carries us, I would like to share with you some events in my life. I am sure they will show the power of surrender.

The Easter Festival of Praise was the start of my understanding of what happens when we trust in the Lord so completely, that we let Him be in charge of a situation.

It was the start of my truly understanding the great gift of surrender.

It was not long after my surrender prayer that I awoke one morning with a scene running through my mind.

I 'saw' members of all the local churches walking in procession through the streets of our local town carrying banners and singing. They were travelling in joyful procession towards the Woodville Halls (the town's civic centre and theatre).

They then assembled inside and praised the Lord together.

Then these words came to me: –

'I want my people to show others the Joy of being a Christian.' and also 'Healing will take place in the preparation.'

I somehow knew that it was Easter Sunday and the time 3.00pm.

It was such a vivid scene that I thought maybe it was the Lord's wish for this to actually happen!

Now, some of you may find the concept of the Lord talking through images in our mind difficult, but it does seem to be the way the Lord speaks to me.

I am also aware that our imagination can play tricks on us, so I asked the Lord to confirm to me that this was from Him and this was His Will.

I said 'Lord if this is from you let someone mention the Woodville Halls to me today.'

But I thought this would be highly unlikely as I was spending most of that day alone.

However, in the evening whilst I was having a meal with my sister-in-law, the conversation turned to the topic of deafness.

'I know someone' she said 'who bought a hearing aid at an exhibition in the **Woodville Halls**.'

My heart started to beat faster 'O Lord' I said 'I think you are telling me to go ahead.'

What do I do now?

I then started to think of how I should go ahead as I had only recently returned to the district and didn't have any contact with members of other denominations.

(I was told later that there was not much contact between the local churches at this time.)

So the next day during Mass I prayed about this, and the thought came to me that I should pay a visit to the Woodville Halls to make sure that it was actually available for hire on the Easter Sunday.

I went along there, quite nervously, wondering what I should say if they were to ask me the reason I wanted to hire their halls.

I thought that they might be rather intrigued by my story.

However, when I arrived there I was rather disappointed to be told that on the Easter Sunday, the halls had already been booked for a Sikh wedding. 'Well maybe' I thought, 'the Lord wants this to take place next year, to give us time to arrange everything.'

So I asked them if it would be available for the following Easter Sunday.

'No' I was told 'that day is also booked for a Sikh wedding'.

In fact the woman continued to explain that nearly every Sunday through the year, had already been booked for either a wedding or for entertainment.

She said that she was very sorry but was only able to offer me a date in June.

She also offered other venues, but I knew that if it wasn't possible to fulfil all the details given to me, then this was not from the Lord.

Then, as the woman was looking in her diary and suggesting Easter Monday to me, she suddenly said 'Oh, the person who booked the halls for this Easter Sunday hasn't paid his deposit yet and we told him a month ago, that if he didn't pay this by today, we would have to cancel his booking. I'll telephone him at lunchtime to ask him what he intends to do and then ring you this afternoon with the answer.'

'O Lord' I thought 'I am sure that you have made this man reserve this date, knowing that he wouldn't need it so that it would be kept free for your purposes.'

I went home and prayed until I received the phone call telling me that the hall was ours and then I went straight down to the office and paid my deposit.

I was so sure that this was indeed from the Lord that I surrendered the whole thing to Him, asking Him to be in charge, but knowing deep inside me that there was no need to worry.

As I knew in the depth of my heart that this all belonged to Him, and my part was to pray and to be led, I decided to pray for a month without doing anything more.

The visits begin...

After the month, at the suggestion of members of my prayer group, I went to the library to get a list of all the local vicars, priests and pastors in the area.

There were over thirty!

I decided to contact the first one on the list, and when we met I asked if we could pray together for the Holy Spirit to guide our words and thoughts. After the prayer, I told him of the 'vision' that I felt the Lord had given to me.

He seemed interested but was rather non-committal (in fact the Canon of this church who usually made the decisions, was ill at the time) and suggested that I should contact another local pastor.

So I made an appointment and went to see him. We met and after we had prayed together I shared the 'vision'

This pastor received it much more enthusiastically than the previous one – that is until he learned that I was a Catholic. I had not had much involvement with other denominations, and was quite taken aback that I should be dismissed for being a Catholic. I told him, 'I don't come as a Catholic but because I feel the Lord has asked me to do so.'

'Well', he said, 'I must pray about this' I felt that he was unsure of what to do as he somehow felt that the message was authentic. I later learned that he had wanted to arrange such a meeting himself but had been unable to do so because the Halls were all booked!

I would like to add here that this particular pastor became very dear to me and was one of the greatest supporters.

God is good!

I then went on to contact others on the list and was received well in some cases, with suspicion from others, but we always prayed together.

However no one seemed to want to make a commitment.

Suddenly it was January and Easter was in April and by this time I had only been able to contact about half of the leaders of the churches, so I was advised that I should write to the remainder and invite them to a meeting.

This was to be arranged for the end of January.

Lord am I doing this right?

In the meantime my brother, a married Deacon, very enthusiastic and supportive of the Easter Festival, said that he thought it would be a good idea to speak about all this at a forthcoming Deanery meeting.

He thought that perhaps the clergy would like to help with some advertising material and posters.

However, this worried me, as I felt that this would present the event as coming from the Catholic Church and that it was they, who were inviting the other Christians to attend.

I knew that this festival belonged to all Christians.

There was another aspect that I was also worried about.

I did not want to dampen my brother's enthusiasm by disagreeing with his suggestion; after all he is my elder brother and is also a member of the clergy.

So to soften my refusal I said that maybe I needed some advice and perhaps I should contact a *Canon lawyer*, to confirm that I was following the right course.

(I had never used those words before).

Within a few hours another of my brothers, who lives in Austria, telephoned me and said 'Veronica, you would have loved the retreat I have just been on, there was a *Canon lawyer* there from Rome and his talk was wonderful' When I asked him 'did you tell him about the Easter Festival of Praise' he replied 'I did and he said

"This is from the Holy Spirit – Praise the Lord, Praise the Lord".'

What a quick and marvellous answer to my request, the Lord always gives me the top man!

Meeting the others...

When our meeting for members of all the different denominations took place I noticed that there were very few clergy there, but they had sent their representatives.

We started with a prayer and then I was asked to share the 'vision'. When I had finished, it was suggested that we should form a committee to make arrangements for the event. However one leader disagreed and said 'the Lord has given this to Veronica, I think she should be in charge.'

My heart sank as I had thought my part was only to tell the vision to others!

Then he suggested that we should all pray again, and have a time of silence to listen to the Lord.

During this quiet time a woman from the Baptist church stood up, breaking the silence as she prayed 'Lord I repent for all the bad feelings that I have had in the past towards Catholics'. Then one by one, other people stood up and prayed a similar prayer.

I too, asked for forgiveness for my arrogance in the past, towards my fellow Christians.

Then I remembered, with joy, the Lord's words at the beginning 'Healing will take place in the preparation.' He had honoured His promise!

Because we felt that this was the Lord's work, we decided that we would not have a committee but we would meet every week in a different church and praise Him.

We would not initiate anything ourselves, we would meet together, pray, praise and listen and then wait to follow His directives.

We were not at all worried that we only had a few weeks to the event – we just knew that if this was in His Will and we firmly believed it was, He had everything in place.

We had great peace.

During this meeting members of the Anglican Church had offered to take charge of the music, and a member of the Full Gospel church, his help to a Catholic member to design some posters.

And at the end of this meeting, we made a decision to meet the following Monday to pray and praise together in the Anglican Church.

The music group is formed...

We had invited anyone with a musical talent to join the music ministry and those who wished, to join the choir.

When we met the following week we were truly amazed as we listened to the musicians, most of whom had never played together before. Their music was truly wonderful.

As we prayed together we stared to feel excited at the thought of what lay ahead and what the Lord had in store for us.

We now had our choir and our musicians, but wondered what would happen next?

Well, we just continued to meet and praise the Lord each week quite unworried as we knew that He was in charge.

Now, you want drama, Lord?

Then five weeks before the event, one of our members told us that when she prayed the rosary, the words came to her 'Walk my son's life'. She asked us what we thought it meant. At the time it didn't mean anything special to us.

However, it all became very clear a few days later.

It was on the evening after the meeting in the Baptist church, when a sales representative called at her house and unusually she didn't have her order ready for him. So she invited him into her house, and asked him to wait while she wrote it out.

She was still so excited about the previous evening, and told him what a wonderful time it had been and then told him all about our proposed Easter Festival of Praise.

'I know' was his reply 'I was there last night too.'

Then this woman's daughter came into the room and said that she had seen this man there and for some reason she had thought of drama. It was all very strange because he then told her that when he had seen her, he too had thought of drama.

The mother was so excited when she telephoned me to tell me all this and said she really thought that the Lord was speaking through them.

My thought was 'Lord, I know nothing about drama, and we have only five weeks before the event, how can we arrange this?'

But the next morning, as I awoke I began to understand the words 'walk my son's life' Of course, that was it! At our Easter Festival we should not just praise God for the Resurrection of His Son, but also for His whole life – starting with the angel's visit to Mary, right up to His Resurrection!

It then became very clear to me that we should have short scenes from the life of Jesus, accompanied by a Scripture reading and a song to praise each event.

My heart was filled with joy, as I knew this was to be!

Then suddenly the thought that I knew nothing about drama hit me again, 'But where, Lord, will I find someone who knows about drama?' I asked.

However all was well, as I discovered later that day when I visited my mother in the nursing home. The doctor who was attending her, asked me about the progress for the Festival.

I told him what was on my mind and that I thought the Lord wanted us to include drama, but I admitted that I just did not know where to start.

The sister of the ward overheard our conversation and said that she knew of a nurse who worked there and was involved in drama.

So I asked her when this nurse would next be on duty, and she told me that she would be there the next day.

I was rather nervous when I went to see her, as I was wondering just how to approach her – after all, she would probably think me a bit strange when I said that I thought it was *the Lord* who had asked for this event.

So I decided to start by asking her if she was a Christian and was very relieved when she said 'yes.'

I then asked her if she had seen the posters in the church about the Easter Festival of Praise.

I was disappointed when she said 'No' but decided to be brave and to tell her everything that had happened and related the whole story to her.

As I did so, her mouth started to fall open in disbelief as if she were completely surprised by all that was being said.

She told me that three years before, she had wanted to stage the life of Christ but no one had been interested.

But why she was so amazed was because at that time, she too had thought that members of the local churches would attend, and they would come in procession through the streets to the Woodville Halls for the performance.

The Lord had prepared her heart three years before.

She then told me that she was very much involved in drama, and was one of the leading members of the local Arts council and said that it was actually most unusual for her not to have any work at that time.

She was not only one of the most experienced people in drama in the area; she also had contact with the lighting experts and knew everyone who worked at the Halls.

As I have said before the Lord always gives us the best.

Who will read the Scriptures?

So we spoke at length about what I felt the Lord wanted and she agreed but added that it was important to have people who were good at reading Scripture.

She said she did know of a couple who would be ideal but was doubtful that they would be available because it would be the Easter weekend and they would probably be on holiday.

The next day I received a telephone call from her and she told me excitedly that now she knew that this was truly from the Lord: because these people are not only free for that weekend and willing to be involved, but had just returned from a course on how to read the Scriptures!

The Lord had surely prepared everything.

So, five weeks before the event our programme had started to take shape.

I was happy to leave the drama presentation to this woman.

I had nothing to fear, nothing to check on, and felt that I could leave everything to her as I was sure that the Lord had chosen her.

Lord, we know that you will show us what else you want!

About this time, I was asked by a Pastor, 'Who is going to be the preacher?' 'I don't know' I replied 'but if there is to be a preacher the Lord already has one in mind.'

I had learned by this time that He is the best organiser and that He had everything in place.

Although we still did not know what else the Lord wanted in His programme, we carried on praying and praising every Monday and we became very close to each other, excited by what was happening.

About this time, my brother asked me if I would like him to bring a group from Hungary, to be part of the Festival. Evidently one of them, a young girl, had experienced a wonderful healing from drugs, alcohol and self-mutilation.

The Lord had healed her instantly of all addiction, and without any withdrawal symptoms. Because of this she had given her life to the Lord and felt that now He wanted her to witness to this miracle through mime around the world.

Now, I was not sure if this would be suitable for our Festival, but I did promise to pray about it.

If they have something to say, let them speak.

It was just three weeks before the event, that I had another telephone call from my brother. This time he said that he would like to bring the group anyway, as he had room in the car and they wanted to come as part of the audience.

Our programme was still incomplete, so I said to him that I would pray again about whether they should take part or not.

I returned to my prayers and asked the Lord to help me and show me what He wanted.

When I opened the Bible – the words before me were amazing. I can't remember the exact passage I think it must have been from Acts because the words were that 'if they have something to tell about the glory of the Lord, let them stand in front of the assembly and declare it.'

For me this was the confirmation I needed – our programme was now complete!

As it became closer to the date of our Festival we began to wonder how many people would come. We only had a few of the clergy openly supporting us, but we were all still very peaceful about it.

My sister remarked that she felt that even if no one turned up on the day, the wonderful spirit of unity we had all experienced during the preparation was enough.

A rehearsal for the drama had been arranged for Maundy Thursday. Well, if we had not been reliant on the Lord, I am sure we would have been very worried at this stage. With only three days to go we did not have enough people, we only had two apostles, and the acting was, to say the least, not impressive.

But we were all so calm.

It is difficult to describe how we felt – just full of peace, feeling privileged to be taking part in His plan.

Even the woman in charge of the drama was unruffled. Somehow we knew that the responsibility was not in our hands.

Prayers for protection.

The day before the event we had decided that we would pray for protection and walk over every route the people would take from their respective churches to the Halls.

On that morning, during prayer, a rather strange "picture" came to my mind, which I did not understand and which did not seem to have any relevance.

It was of a stagecoach being pulled by galloping horses with steam coming out of their nostrils. There was a large catapult dominating the picture, which was aimed at the horses, in a threatening way.

I just did not understand this picture at all.

Later that day we did our prayer walk over all the routes, praying for protection as we went. Then to my amazement when we reached the Halls, there in front of me was a full size papier mache *stage coach and horses*!

The horses were separated from the stagecoach, as if at the end of a journey. They must have just been used for a stage production.

I knew then, what the Lord had been saying through my picture:

'Don't worry, even though everything now seems to be so rushed with so much to do and even under threat – ALL IS WELL!

On the day everything will be fine. Look at the stage coach – it has reached its destination and those horses are resting.'

What a wonderful God. He knew that we needed re-assurance at that time.

It was just another sign of the Lord's closeness.

So the great day came.

By now, we were all good friends, having met and prayed together for the last six weeks. There was an air of excitement about the place as we still continued to pray for the Lord's will to be done.

Miraculously, extra people came to offer their help for the drama, and rehearsals quickly took place, and although hurried there was still a wonderful feeling of calm.

But we still wondered if anyone would come to the festival.

We did know that there would be at least forty – that was the number in the choir and those taking part.

It had been decided that we would start praising at 2.45pm, so that when the people arrived, they would come into an atmosphere of Praise.

Then, when I looked out of the main door at ten minutes to three, I nearly cried with joy. What a wonderful sight! Groups of Christians were coming down the streets in procession, waving banners, smiling and happy full of joy and coming from all directions.

Filled to capacity ... blessings and conversions.

The Halls had a capacity for eight hundred people including the crèche and that was the number who came!

All denominations were represented and even the Mayor of the town came too.

How great it is when the Lord is in charge.

And what a wonderful afternoon it proved to be.

The Hall was filled with Christians, singing and praising and even dancing in the aisles. They were so happy as they praised the Lord together.

The drama was so good that it was difficult to believe that these were the same people we had seen just three days before. The ones who had come at the last minute, knowing we were short of actors to offer their help, acted as though they had been with us throughout the preparations and we had the full complement of Apostles!

I was even asked 'where did you get the drama group?'

They were surprised when I told them that the 'actors' were just friends from the local community and members of our families.

The music ministry was excellent (of course Our Lord always gives us the best).

The musicians included an internationally famous harpist, professional violinists, as well as a trumpet player who had only recently decided to attend his local church.

The Lord's timing is perfect!

The Lord uses the weak to witness to His power.

The mime from the people from Hungary was so moving that many people were brought to tears – it gave such a great witness to the power of the Lord.

People told us later that they had experienced a real closeness of the Lord and to each other during that afternoon. One man even asked to speak from the stage. He told us 'I have been looking for happiness all my life and what I see here in you today, is what I have been looking for. Yes, I have found it here today.' He later joined one of the local churches.

I heard of another young man who had a conversion experience and he is now training to be a missionary.

It was certainly a day to remember – not just because of the Joy it had brought to us, but also for the lesson we had learned: that if we let go and let God be God, He will show us His power.

(Our part must always be to pray and then respond).

He certainly showed His Power that day, for how could a few Christians, who had planned nothing, but had met, prayed and praised each week, achieve such a wonderful successful event in just a few weeks?

This is the power of surrender!

Many people afterwards asked me if I would arrange another Festival for the following year. They were all so excited by the afternoon of Praise that they wanted it repeated. Now here I was in a dilemma. I knew that the wonderful day had all been because the Lord had led it and that it was His Will. Did He want this repeated? I did not know.

It did seem that there should be some follow up but I knew that unless this came from Him it would not be a success. I prayed about it and at times felt that maybe I should be doing something more.

However the answer came a few months later when a Methodist friend of mine invited me to a 'Churches Together' meeting.

This was introduced by a local vicar who opened the meeting by saying 'the Lord wants us to meet and pray together as He showed us at the 'Easter Festival of Praise'

I knew then that the follow up was in place and my part done! I had great peace.

This event, I now know, was the training ground for my future work.

Let Go and Let God Be GOD

3. 'Mothers Prayers'

I am sure the experience of the Easter Festival helped me to prepare for this ministry.

Many of you reading this book, I am sure, will already know of 'Mothers Prayers', but for those of you who don't, I will give you some background details.

How we started.

Over a period of time, I. had felt a growing desire to pray in a more committed way for children. Two things happened which confirmed my decision to do so. I had became involved with the Maranatha community and they had produced a booklet called 'What on earth are we doing to our children?'

This booklet contained horrifying statistics about all the dangers that face our children today. It gave the statistics and also their source. I was present with the group who took it to the House of Lords to bring it to the attention of the ministers.

I heard that some of them found it too difficult to read. This took place in 1995 and I can't help wondering what the booklet would contain if it were written today!

My reaction then was to think 'What kind of society are my nine grandchildren growing up in?' I wanted to do something but felt so helpless and small compared to all the great problems that this booklet highlighted.

But deep inside me I knew that the answer was to PRAY.

About this time my sister in law told me that she had been awakened in the night on two occasions with the words 'Pray for your children'.

The first time that it had happened was when she was at Walsingham taking part in the New Dawn conference. As the organisers had arranged all night prayer vigils, she got up and went to the Chapel to pray. But later when she returned home, the same thing happened. She told me that she really felt that the Lord was speaking to her about the need to pray for children.

We decided then that this was what we must do and so we prayed every day for a month asking the Lord to guide us. We were certain that the prompting had come from Him.

We asked Him to show us what to do and said 'Lord you are the Boss and we will be your secretaries'.

From my past experience I knew that this was the safest and most wise thing to do!

A good secretary has to wait for the boss's instruction. I knew for sure, that the best way forward was to surrender the whole thing to the Lord and ask Him to be in charge.

We knew that our part would be to pray and that He would lead us and open up the doors.

I certainly see now how the Lord has honoured this surrender – it is impossible for two grandmothers in their own strength to achieve the wonderful things that have happened since we started.

'Mothers Prayers' is now in most major countries around the world. We have contacts in over eighty countries and there are thousands of groups and all this in just eight years.

One of the most amazing things we have experienced is the way it has spread around the world without us initiating any publicity ourselves – *He* has brought the people to *us*. We only ever go to give talks to groups or visit countries when we are invited – He knows the priorities and whom we should visit first.

The Lord is surely the best publicity agent.

Sometimes people ask how did it spread around the world if you didn't arrange any publicity.

Well, our first publicity came soon after our decision to start 'Mothers Prayers' I was asked by a friend if I would give him a lift in my car to Birmingham as he wanted to attend a conference there. I was about to make a journey home to Kent from Manchester, and Birmingham is approximately half way.

When we arrived at the centre my friend asked me if I would like to go to the conference. I was very interested in the subject (Pro-Life) so I readily accepted.

I was then introduced to a friend of his and was asked if I would tell him about Mothers Prayers.

Because the conference was about to start, the conversation I had with him was very brief, but he told me that he was a journalist for the Catholic newspaper, the Universe and asked me if I would mind if he wrote an article about 'Mothers Prayers'.

I was rather surprised but agreed and asked that the article would include an address so that contact could be made if any mother was interested.

The article came out a few weeks later at Christmas and then it appeared in the Church of England newspaper. I was even more surprised when I received a telephone call from a local Baptist minister who had seen the article and asked me if I would speak on Radio Kent.

(There was a wonderful response from mothers from all over the country).

And we had all this publicity just because I gave someone a lift.

How great is our God!

We meet in a train...

It was not long after this that I visited London for a day of sightseeing with a friend from Scotland. We had a wonderful time together. When we were on the train about to travel home, a couple, who by their accent were obviously from overseas, asked us if the train was going to a certain station. When we confirmed that it was indeed the right train they came and sat in our carriage. To make conversation, I asked them if they had been sightseeing. However, it seemed that the gentleman who was from Holland was moving to our district for his work.

As we continued to chat together his wife asked my friend if this was her first visit to London. She told them it was her second visit as she had been before to visit the House of Lords.

She explained that we had gone there with a group of Christians to present the booklet 'What on earth are we doing to our children' (the same booklet that had inspired me to start 'Mothers Prayers') to the Politicians.

The woman seemed concerned at what we were saying and said that she didn't know what could be done to help the situation for children.

Somehow, (I believe it was the Lord) I felt prompted to ask her if she was a Christian. When she replied that she was, I said to her 'then you understand the power of prayer' and told her that we felt that this was the only answer. I then briefly told her about 'Mothers Prayers'.

As I finished she turned to her husband and said 'Now I know why we missed the last train and why we are sitting in this carriage. The Lord has been speaking to me and I haven't been listening. I will take 'Mothers Prayers' to Mexico and Kuwait.'

You see, even though we had thought that we had gone to London for a day of sightseeing, I felt sure that the Lord had arranged for this meeting too.

In the kitchen of a presbytery!...

On another occasion, I went to visit a friend of mine who is a priest, as he wanted to show me his new church and offer me some of the hymn books he no longer required.

Whilst we were talking in his kitchen, he received a call asking him to go and see someone urgently. I felt that he didn't want to leave me alone, because he asked a woman, who was cleaning the church, to come and share a cup of tea with me.

As he left he asked me to tell her about 'Mothers Prayers'

Well, at this time I was very excited as we had just had out first answer to prayer, and so I happily told her about this and all about 'Mothers Prayers'.

Our first answer to prayer...

In our church at this time we had a young visitor from Hungary. She had come to England to work as an au pair. This young woman had offered to help the parishioners in their homes, so that she could raise extra money for her studies.

When she came to our house to do some ironing, I introduced her to my daughter who was helping me with the paperwork for 'Mothers Prayers'. I explained to her the call we felt to pray for children and about our prayer groups.

She then said 'please pray for a friend of mine, she came to England from Hungary also to be an au pair.' It seems that she had not settled here and her mother had sent her the money for her bus fare to return home. Her landlord had taken her to the bus but when it arrived in Hungary the girl was nowhere to be seen. She had apparently disappeared on her way home.

The attempts of the police to trace her had failed and she had now been missing for six months.

I told her that, of course we would pray for her, but as we were a 'Mothers Prayers' group, we would pray on behalf of her mother. We did so that same day, as it was the day for our meeting.

You can imagine how excited we were the next day when we heard that this missing girl had just telephoned her mother in Hungary to say that she was alive and well!

After I had told all this to the woman, as we had our cup of tea in the priest's kitchen, she told me that she was sure that she was meant to meet me, as she didn't usually clean the church on that day and had never stayed so late before.

She said that she was a member of the Union of Catholic Mothers and asked if I would be willing to give them a talk.

A few weeks later, when I met up with her before the arranged meeting, she had some exciting news for me.

She had told her sister all about 'Mothers Prayers' and they had prayed together for her son who had been missing for over four years and he didn't even know that his father had died, and nine days later he came home! Praise the Lord!

The Lord has continued to open the way for us and our part has been the prayer, responding when He gives us the opportunities and leaving Him to arrange the publicity.

The Lord blesses us...

We have heard of so many answers to prayers, since 'Mothers Prayers' started.

These have included big things like children coming off drugs, leaving bad relationships, returning home after they have been missing for several years, returning to their Faith, and many wonderful answers to health problems even when the doctors have said that there was no hope.

Also mothers, who have resisted the advice of doctors to have an abortion because of problems with their expected babies, have given birth to babies who have been born healthy, or have responded well to surgery. We have been told of married couples on the point of separating, or couples already separated, and have now renewed their marriage commitment to each other.

There have been many cases too of young people who had been living together, deciding to get married.

There have been many answers to prayers that, although we might not consider them to be so dramatic, are wonderful for the parents – answers like improved relationships within the family, children who are given a place in the school of their choice in spite of at first being refused, bullying at school that has stopped and just generally more peace in the family.

The blessings have been many for the mothers themselves, even those who have not yet had an answer to their prayers.

They find that by coming together each week, to surrender their children into the care of the Lord and by sharing with other mothers (knowing that it is in total confidence), their pain has been eased. They soon become filled with hope and peace.

For us, it is a wonderful comfort to know that the 'Boss' has all these things in hand. The one worry I sometimes have is that, in my enthusiasm, I might get in His way by trying to take over!

Oops, sorry Lord...

Once, forgetting the surrender, I thought that it would be a good idea to contact a certain women's organisation. But soon the alarm bells went in my head as I remembered that I was only the secretary and not the boss, so I said 'Oops, sorry Lord' and then committed some time to prayer instead.

Later that week a member of this organisation contacted me!

It was the same week of my encounter on the train and also during that same week a woman telephoned me who said that she would take 'Mothers Prayers' to China.

I smiled as I felt the Lord saying 'Thank you for leaving things to me, you might have had some success with the women's organisation, but could you have made contact with Mexico, China and Kuwait?'

Will you trust me with your talks? ...

Right from the beginning, in line with my surrender, I knew that I would have to completely trust in the Lord: so when through prayer I felt that I should not take any notes when I had to give a talk, but speak from the heart, I knew that I had to obey. The first time was in the Baptist church for the Easter Festival of Praise and it was a bit daunting. I wondered what would happen if I couldn't find the right words or if I were to dry up, unable to think of anything to say.

But everything went well and I was told later that the talk could not have been better.

Now I find that through my reliance on Him, I am so much more relaxed. I do not worry before meetings, as I am convinced that He will give me the right words to say. Just before a talk I say 'over to you Lord' and He has always honoured this. He alone knows the needs of the people to whom I am speaking.

This has been so freeing! I am the sort of person that if I had to write a talk myself would agonise over every paragraph. I would keep changing my mind and spend hours over the attempt.

When we were in Brno, in the Czech Republic, I remember being in St Thomas' Church waiting to speak at a quite large gathering (I think there was about 700 people). It was the first time I had spoken through an interpreter, but I was so detached – it was almost as if I were waiting for someone else to speak. And in a way I was, for I asked the Lord to give me the words to say.

When we were invited by the Catholic Archbishop to speak at the meeting in Moscow for the priests and nuns of Russia, I would have been terrified if I had thought that *I* had to prepare the talk. I would probably have been up half the night, trying to do so. Instead I slept well knowing that my part was only to pray and to trust.

The meeting was very blessed and as a result the Archbishop asked for an article to go in the Catholic newspaper of Russia.

It was through this article that we met our co-ordinator for Russia and there are now many, many groups there, both in the Catholic and Russian Orthodox Churches.

And in Brazil last year it was the ultimate test when I had to speak live on Television to an expected audience of 40,000.000 people and for a few sessions and without notes! But the Lord blessed my words.

And He leads us...

It was whilst we were in Russia, that we were very blessed by the Lord (our Boss).

We were due to speak to a group in the Orthodox Church but had time to spare so we decided to have a cup of coffee in McDonalds.

My brother had said that he knew exactly where to go but somehow we got lost – in fact I later found out that we were going in the opposite direction. Our Russian is almost non- existent so although we tried to ask for directions, we were unsure of the reply. At last someone seemed to understand and so we were directed to a church. But it was the Church of England –naturally as we were English they had thought that this was where we would want to go.

We went inside as we thought that there may be someone who would direct us to the Orthodox Church, and found that their service had just ended and they were having tea.

The people were really welcoming and asked us the reason we were in Moscow. We then explained to them all about 'Mothers Prayers'

We left marveling how the Lord had taken us there at exactly the right time – to give us an opportunity to explain our ministry.

We knew that if *we* had decided that it would be a good idea to go to this church to explain about 'Mothers Prayers' we would never have found it, especially at exactly the right time, the end of their service and also when people who were interested in our work would be there.

A similar incident happened in St. Petersburg where we had an encounter with two women at the metro station.

They seemed to be watching us as we were puzzling over a map and they then asked us if they could help (at least that was what we understood from their actions). We pointed to a post office symbol on the map and they shook their heads saying 'niet' (no) and indicated that we should follow them. We dutifully followed them, not knowing quite where we were going, to discover that they had led us to a Post Office much nearer than the one we had marked out for ourselves.

They were smiling all the time and seemed eager to please us. They then gave us some little booklets about St Petersburg.

We were so grateful and the only way I could think to thank them was to give them one of our 'Mothers Prayers' booklets which had been translated into Russian.

I pointed to them and asked 'Christian?' One answered 'niet' but the other 'Da, Baptist'. After they thanked us we left them and went back to our hotel.

We had shown them the brochure of our hotel, so they knew where we were staying, but we were very surprised to receive a phone call from an American lady later who told us she was their translator. She asked us if she could come to see us with the Baptist lady, as she wanted to find out more about 'Mothers Prayers'.

These are just a few examples of how The Lord opened the right doors for us at the right time. Only He knows these things.

He has His plan and provided that we wait in prayer and do not interfere or rush ahead he will put everything in place.

He supplies all our needs…

Something else happened during a visit to Russia that I would like to tell you about, as it will surely illustrate all that I am saying.

It was during our very first visit to Russia. A priest who was a friend of our family had invited my brother and me to stay there for a month.

This was so exciting for us – we had never thought that we would go to Russia. It was one of those places we had prayed for as children, a sort of mysterious place – almost frightening to us. Maybe this was from all the propaganda we heard on the radio and television.

We arrived there in February. It was very cold but very beautiful too. The fir trees were covered in snow and the sun was shining. It felt so wonderful just to be there.

After we had settled in, our friend told us that he was not sure how or when we could talk about 'Mothers Prayers'. He told us of the strict rule, which made it impossible for us to talk outside of the parish, as we could be accused of proselytising.

To make matters worse he told us that he did not have an interpreter.

But I had come to understand that if the Lord takes us anywhere, He would have everything in place. I just said quite confidently, 'We'll pray Father.'

Later as I was praying in his private chapel, before the Blessed Sacrament thanking the Lord for bringing us safely to Russia and also asking for an interpreter, the door opened and a woman came in and naturally, spoke to me in Russian.

'Sorry' I said 'I am English.' She then answered me in perfect English – she was in fact a teacher of English.

What really amazed me was the fact that this was her first visit to the church even though she had lived in the town all her life. I later found out that she was a Jew.

She had come to the church to see if there was anyone who would help her study the Bible, but when she found the church was locked, she had walked round the back and had found this private chapel.

I said 'I think I know why you are here'.

Yes, she became our interpreter!

Our God is so mighty! We had prayed for an interpreter and one walked through the door!

Why has 'Mothers Prayers' been so powerful? I truly believe that is because it belongs to the Lord, and as we accept this and trust in Him, it is as if He says to us 'Now you are beginning to understand – you must leave everything to Me'.

We surrender our **children...**

We feel the Lord is pleased too with the way we surrender our children to Him in our prayer groups.

For those who have not been involved with 'Mothers Prayers' let me explain.

Each week, after we have said our prayers of preparation from our little booklet, the prayers inviting the Holy Spirit to inspire our meetings, asking for protection, praising and acknowledging the majesty of God, and reading from Scripture, we unite our prayers with all 'Mothers Prayers' groups around the world (a mighty prayer army!)

Then the most important part of our meeting follows, when one by one, we kneel at the table and place the names of our children, at the foot of the cross, acknowledging that we cannot do anything to change their lives but we know that He can.

As we offer our child into His care, we will say a little prayer from the heart.

Our prayer will be something like this; 'Lord I know that you love my child far more than I could possibly love him, he belongs to You more than to me, and you can change things that I can't. So I place him now into your care'

(This is another part of our surrender. We ask God to be God not only of our lives but also in the lives of our children.)

We have learned not to worry so much because we give our problems to Him and always try to remind ourselves not to take them back again!

We remember His Promise in Matthew 7 'Ask and you *shall receive*' and also His invitation 'Come to Me all you who labour and are heavy burdened and I will give you rest' in Matthew 11.

We have seen too, how the Lord is using Mothers Prayers for Christian unity.

It is so wonderful to see mothers from all denominations and fellowships praying together including Catholic and Orthodox women in Russia!

As we join together in prayer for our children, we lovingly accept each other thinking only on everything that unites us, leaving the Holy Spirit to change the things that still separate. Barriers have definitely been broken down and misunderstandings have been cleared away. I am sure that we understand even more that we must pray for Jesus' prayer to the Father to become a reality in our lives.

'Father, that they may be one as You and I are one'. (Jn 17:21)

We have been given so many wonderful examples of the power of surrender that I will never, ever doubt that this is one of the most sensible things I have ever done in my life

If you would like to know more about Mothers Prayers please visit our website www.mothersprayers.org

4. Moving office.

As 'Mothers Prayers' grew, it soon became obvious that I would need a new office. The one I was using was formerly the porch way to my house and was only big enough for a computer, a desk and filing cabinet. It was very difficult for two people to be in there at one time.

So I started to ask around to see if anyone knew of an office that I could use, but without success. I thought that perhaps my priest may have some space in his office but he was unable to help, as he actually needed more room himself.

A solution...

One day, after one of our 'Mothers Prayers' meetings, one of our members told me that she knew of a couple who attended her local Anglican church, who were looking for a smaller place to live. She wondered if we might like to exchange homes.

I knew where they lived so went to look at the outside of their bungalow, however I quickly dismissed it, as it really did not look any bigger than my own.

But the Lord had other ideas!

A few weeks later, I was approached by a woman and although I did not know her very well, I knew that she was the owner of the bungalow – the one that I had already decided was not right for me.

She said that she hoped I didn't mind her asking me something. She said that she had just returned from a retreat at the Carmelite Monastery at Aylesford in Kent and at the end of this retreat it had been suggested to her that she should have a Spiritual director and to consider having one who was a Catholic.

She said that she had prayed about this and felt the Lord had put it into her mind to ask me!

I was very surprised by this – it certainly was not the sort of thing that anyone would expect from someone they did not know too well.

I explained to her that I had no formal training but if the Lord had put this on her heart, then I was willing to meet with her.

Because I was rather embarrassed, I changed the subject by asking if she had sold her house. She looked at me in surprise and asked 'How did you know we were thinking of moving?'

So I told her of the conversation that had taken place with our mutual friend.

Then she asked me if I was still thinking of moving. So I told her that I did expect to move at some stage, as now my bungalow was not big enough, but said that because I had given my life to the Lord, I could only move when He wished.

Thankfully, she seemed to understand this.

Can we see your house?...

I was quite surprised when a week or so later she telephoned me to say that she had looked at the outside of my house and could she come with her husband to see the inside.

I didn't say that I had already seen her house and thought that it would not be suitable. But I thought I had better be open to her suggestion, as after all I was now supposed to be her Spiritual director!

So they came to view, and looking back I feel that I did rather rush them around, as in my mind I was so sure that I would not be moving in the near future.

They then invited me to look at their bungalow.

I must say that it was much larger inside than it had looked from the outside.

I did think it was nice but I didn't think the Lord would want me there somehow.

I had imagined that when I moved, it would be to a big rundown house that we would have to renovate.

Sometimes we don't expect the Lord to give us better things.

(This was another new lesson that I had to learn).

So I told my new friends that, as I had mentioned before, I would only move if I felt it was what the Lord wished and said 'why don't we pray about it, together.'

The Lord was paving the way...

I should mention here, that at a prayer meeting on the previous day, I felt that the Lord had given me a 'picture'.

It was of a big pot, like a cauldron, and into this pot articles such as keys, purses and other items were being thrown.

I said to the members of our group 'I think the Lord is saying put all your worries into my pot of Love.' So one by one, we prayed 'Lord, into the pot I put.....' and mentioned our needs.

Now, the very next day, when I suggested to the owners of the house that we should pray together, the husband replied 'Shall we put it into the prayer pot?'

I was absolutely amazed and said 'You don't know what you have just said' and I explained to him that the day before, we were all putting things into the 'prayer pot'. His wife said that he had never, ever, used that expression before!

They were as surprised as I.

I thought 'Oh, Oh, Lord I think that perhaps you do want me to come here after all'.

After this, there were other confirmations, including one from my brother.

I had told him that I thought the Lord was asking me to move and when he asked me where, I told him that it was still in the same area. Then he asked me the name of the street, but before I told him he said 'I know the name of the street. It has just come into my mind' and he was right!

The next step...

So we considered what we should do next. And then felt that we should get a valuation from a local agent for both properties and we agreed that we would accept his valuation whatever we personally thought.

Well, his valuation was that their property was worth £40,000 more than mine.

So I said, Lord if you want me to move I need £40,000!

Later my prayer partner telephoned me and told me that I was not to worry as she had asked the Lord for £45,000. That was the £40,000 for the house and £5,000 for the Russian visit. (I had invited some Russian friends to stay for a month.)

As soon as we had finished our conversation, I looked to the floor and there I discovered a £5 note.

I had not noticed it before and I still don't know how it got there, but it did become significant to me later.

I said 'Lord, if you are going to give this money to me in £5's, it's going to take a really long time!'

I then decided to approach the building society and asked them for the cheapest way to borrow this money. To borrow such an amount at that time would have cost in the region of £400 per month

The woman at the building society then told me of a new law that had just been introduced. This enabled people over fifty five years of age, to borrow money on an interest only basis. So by taking my old mortgage (which was quite considerable) and then adding the extra £40,000 my additional repayment instead of £400 per month was just an extra £40.

I have a sneaking suspicion that this law had been brought in at this time just for me.

(Later the interest rate went down again and the additional sum became even less).

The building society also had a special promotion. It was for customers who had needed additional finance and remained loyal to their company. They were to be given £250 as a loyalty payment, so I qualified for this.

I was then told that there was a surveyor's fee to be paid and this was £255. So all I needed was an additional £5. I smiled as I thought of the £5 I had found on the carpet!

Will you leave all behind?...

After I had sorted out the financial situation, I often met and prayed with the couple who were exchanging homes with me. It was after one of these visits that the wife told me 'When we were leaving here last time I felt the Lord say 'furniture', how do you feel about leaving your furniture behind and taking ours?'

My first thought was 'this is not so easy' after all I had chosen all this furniture and it was to my taste. However I didn't hesitate too long and said 'If you think that this is what the Lord wants, then I agree.'

It did make sense after all the decor and size of the rooms were so different and each had suitable furniture.

Then later, when I was looking at the display cabinets which held all my china that I had collected over the years, I thought, 'They look so right in that cabinet, Lord do you want me to leave those too?'.

I went to pray and then opened my Bible – it opened at the page that quoted 'Leave everything behind' so that is what I did.

We left everything, furniture, beds, bedding, linen, crockery, and kitchen utensils – everything except personal belongings.

It was only later, when I had moved to the new house that I discovered that all their cupboards were crammed full of china, glasses, dishes etc. In fact everything we would need for our community.

Our God is never outdone in generosity.

Also by leaving everything behind I was given a great freedom but I only realised this after I had moved into the new house.

One of our members had been washing up and had accidentally broken a milk jug. 'Veronica' she said apologetically 'I have broken the jug' 'Oh, the waste bin is over there' I replied.

It was then that I realised that if it had been one from my best collection, I would have been upset at the loss. The crockery in the new house meant nothing to me and so it was easy to let go.

We had started to move our personal things long before the contracts were exchanged – as we all knew that this move belonged to the Lord.

The husband had the keys of my bungalow and moved the personal things whilst I was away giving talks for 'Mothers Prayers'.

Wow, Lord all I asked for was a bigger office!...

When I was sitting in my new home just three months after I had first met the previous owners, I marveled at how it had all happened.

I thought 'I am sitting here in a house twice the size of the last one, with everything I need, I haven't had the worry of looking for a house, or of showing people around mine (so often there are time wasters or people who do not keep appointments). It has cost me nothing for the surveyor, or for removals, and all I have to pay is a few extra pounds each month! I did not even have to do any packing, only the personal things.'

Our God is so wonderful! Yes, all I had asked for was an office.

And as I looked at the layout of the new house it was if it had been designed for our purposes. It had a prayer room, large office, a kitchen and toilet all together in one section. Then there was a very large lounge, which could be used as a prayer room for when all the prayer groups met and in the third section there were two bedrooms and a bathroom for guests, and finally right at the end of the corridor was my bedroom and bathroom. I am sure that when the house extensions were made, the Lord had put it into the minds of the designers to make it ready for our use. It could not have been better!

The start of the community...

Soon after I moved in – the wife of one of our members came to join us as she felt called to offer help with the gardening. Two more came to help in the office and others with practical offers of help in the house.

Then one day my brother visited me with a fellow Deacon, who told me that he had prepared a dinner party for friends the day before, as he loved cooking! Jokingly I said that I wished I had known that, as twenty four people had recently come to the house for a time of prayer and for a meal.

He then said 'Oh I would love to cook for you'.

So after this, every time we had visitors, he not only cooked for us but also planned and shopped for us too!

The Lord had given us everything we needed.

At this stage one of our group said 'we are the 'Solace Community'.

The house had been called 'Solace' even before the previous owners moved there.

'Solace' was such an apt name too, for our ministry.

It was as though we had become 'community' without planning it.

Again, I experienced the feeling that the Lord had put everything in place, a long time before we had said 'Yes'.

So we decided to have a weekend of prayer to seek the Lord's will regarding our being 'community' and at the end of the weekend we were left in no doubt. The answer was 'YES' – so we became the 'Solace Community'.

I had much to learn about 'community'.

It was more difficult than I had imagined it would be, even to let go of my privacy.

I found it very difficult initially, to have people coming in and out of 'my' house.

I do tend to be a person who likes to be organised and have a routine.

I had to change in order to accommodate the needs of those who came and to respond to the new demands made on me.

It certainly was a new way of living.

I also found it was difficult to leave the keys of the house with others when I travelled abroad and had to learn not to worry that doors may be left unlocked or the alarm not put on properly.

But there were so many blessings and we all grew together and became closer to each other as we worked and prayed together.

Yes, during this time we grew as a community and our prayer groups grew too.

On the move again...

Before long this house had started to become too small and with the regular visitors we began to have parking problems because the road outside was rather narrow.

When I moved to this house, I had thought that we would be staying there forever. But now it had become clearer to me that we were being called to be a community – to have a centre where some of us could live, and work and pray together.

The International aspect of 'Mothers Prayers' had expanded so rapidly that it was easy to understand why a very wise Irish priest had said 'The one worry I have with 'Mothers Prayers' is that it is growing so quickly it may get out of control.' I felt that now the Lord was putting on my heart the need for a training centre for all

'Mothers Prayers' co-ordinators, so that they could have the support and guidance they needed for their ministry and so we would all remain in His will.

And I knew that as we had contacts now in over eighty countries, it would be impossible for me to visit them all.

I now realise that the first house where the Lord had taken us, had been a necessary step to learn the first stage of being 'community'.

Where do you want us to go Lord?...

As usual we put all this to prayer and so when, some time later, a free newspaper came through the door with a picture of a house on the front page, I immediately felt drawn to it.

'That would be ideal' I thought.

The fact that it was far more than I could afford didn't really sink in. I telephoned the estate agent about it before I went off to Russia.

When I returned, included with my post was the brochure of this rather large house displaying the price quite clearly.

'What on earth was I thinking of to even consider this' I wondered.

However, as I looked through the pages I was astonished to see a statue of Our Lady of Lourdes in the garden. I thought 'they must be Christians' as it is most unusual to see a religious statue in a private garden

So I wondered if the Lord wanted me to go and see this property and decided to pray about it.

My sister was visiting me at the time, and we decided that if it were possible to view the property within one hour, we would go, but if this was not possible, I would drop the whole idea. Somehow it did not seem likely that we would be able to make an appointment so quickly.

So when the answer came back that we could go immediately we set off to view the house, not knowing quite what to expect.

This is it!...

Well, as soon as we got there we felt that this was indeed the right place, and when I felt comfortable to do so, I asked the owner if he was a Christian and his reply was 'very much so'.

He told us that he had been in the house for over fifty years and it had been the family home for him, his wife and their eight children. He told me that he felt reluctant to leave and was only doing so, because the house was now too big and the garden too large.

He told me that he and members of his prayer group had been praying that the house would be bought and used for Christian purposes.

So both our prayers seemed to be on the point of being answered!

The gardens were absolutely beautiful, with many interesting paths and areas, just the right place for prayer.

The house was full of character, in need of modernisation, but we were happy about this, as we would need to make it suitable for our needs.

The way forward...

All this seemed wonderful, but we still did not know how we were going to raise the money to pay for it.

We reported back to the community and in turn they all came to see the property and gave their approval, some rather reluctantly as they were disappointed that we would be leaving the area.

We continued to pray about this and it still felt right that we should pursue the matter.

I suppose I had originally thought that some of us would sell our homes and buy the centre together. I realise now that this would not be feasible as we all have families and we are mostly of pensionable age. It would be senseless to sell our properties and then become a burden to the community as we became older.

Another suggestion was that we should ask any member of 'Mothers Prayers' if they were able, to lend us some money interest free. But I did not feel happy in my spirit about this. (We had never before asked our members for money. Any money we had received had always been by way of donations by those who were able to afford to do so).

Then I thought that I would raise the money as a mortgage against a warehouse I owned. I did actually arrange this, with some difficulty, but somehow I still did not feel at peace.

Then one day during prayer I felt that I should sell the warehouse and donate the money to the charity to buy the centre.

This seemed so right! At last I had peace, although it was quite a big thing to consider, this being my main source of income, which had supported the charity ever since it had started.

I just felt that this was what the Lord was asking me to do.

So I placed the warehouse on the market having put my house up for sale three months before this.

The house and the warehouse are sold...

As a community we had decided to have a special day of prayer about the sale of these properties and around mid-day, whilst we were praying, a young man came to see the house and decided that he would like to buy it.

And an hour later I received a telephone call to say that the warehouse had been sold too. In fact two people wanted the warehouse, so they bid against each other with the result that I received enough extra money to pay all legal costs.

God is so good!

Sometimes people have said to me that they felt that I was good to be able to let go of my financial security. But after I had surrendered, I felt that everything I owned belonged to the Lord anyway and so if He wanted me to sell the warehouse to buy the centre, then that was fine by me. We are after all only stewards of His money and I really feel that the Lord had put everything in place years before; in readiness for the time we would need the money to buy the centre.

Certainly, there were times when I have asked 'Are you sure Lord, this is what you want?' 'Please don't let me go down the wrong path'.

In fact one day I said, 'Lord, I really would like a definite answer because I don't want to go ahead if this is not right'.

On that day we had a visitor from Malta. She had come to attend our 'Mothers Prayers' meeting. Naturally, she did not know that one of the neighbours had been rather annoyed about the cars that were parking in the street. Our visitor had parked her car opposite this woman's car and this had made it impossible for any larger vehicle to drive between them.

We had just started the prayer meeting when we heard a tremendous commotion outside.

It was the sound of car horns being impatiently used. I immediately thought it must be something to do with us and so I went outside. At first I didn't realise that one of the offending cars, which was blocking the road, belonged to our visitor.

But once I knew this, I quickly assured everyone that we would move it immediately. However the driver of the coach wouldn't hear of it and said 'you leave your car where it is, it is not your car but that old...***'s car over there. It's her car that is blocking the road and she is refusing to move it'

It was some time before peace was restored and I knew then that our days there were numbered. It seems that some people do not take kindly to houses being used for prayer meetings, especially when it causes parking problems.

There was another confirmation from the Lord that I just could not ignore.

Let me explain; two years previously, we had felt called to set up an organisation to help young people called 'Children of Faith'. As I have a son in law who likes to write songs, I decided to give him this challenge. 'Write a song that will let the children understand that it really 'is cool' to follow Jesus'. It seems, that when they get to a certain age, their friends persuade them that it is 'not cool' to go to church.

My son in law came back with a very catchy tune with several lines in it, which although they did not really appear to tie up together, my brother explained that this seems to be what young people like

The tune was good and there were many one-liners giving a good message (not too 'holy' that it might put some young people off from singing it.)

Now two years later, on this day when I was asking the Lord for a confirmation whether to go ahead with the purchase of the property, a line from the pop tune my son in law had written, flashed through my mind.

It was *'room at the Inn, don't close the door.'*

These words were written long before we had even thought of moving house!

The new house that we were considering to buy was previously an *Inn* and the reason for us wanting to move was *for more room*. So I knew the Lord was saying through this *'Don't close the door.'*

Incidentally there were other lines from the song, which referred to the house, and of which my son in law had no idea, when he wrote it.

One of them was, 'following that great big Star'

The house is called Star house and each year, a huge star with over forty light bulbs hangs from the roof at Christmas and shines out all over the surrounding countryside.

A great feeling of peace came over me. You see, when the Lord makes His will so clear in ways like this, I am sure you can understand that it is not so difficult to follow His leadings.

You may be interested to know that when my sister in law and I prayed for a month before we started 'Mothers Prayers' we chose to meditate on the third joyful mystery of the Rosary – The birth of Jesus. Since then there have been many wonderful ways that this event, the Nativity, has been used as confirmations for us and we feel that Star House is a place where people can come to meet with Jesus.

What has happened since…

Soon after we arrived at our new centre, we had our first international conference for coordinators.

We had representatives from Belgium, Belarus, Czech Republic, France, Germany, Holland, Ireland, Malta, Russia, Slovak Republic, Ukraine, and from the North of England, together with five priests, from Ireland, Malta, Slovakia, Czech and Russia.

Our Bishop came to visit us here too, during this time.

The reason for the conference had been so that everyone would truly understand the spirituality of our community and the vision given to us for 'Mothers Prayers'.

All the co-ordinators were very happy at the end of the conference and thanked us as they left, saying that they felt so much better equipped and they seemed more enthusiastic to fulfil the role in their country. A great feeling of unity had developed during the week as they shared their experiences, and certainly it was the start of many new friendships.

This was followed by other visitors from abroad including Brazil, Portugal, Australia, New Zealand and Singapore and also many members from this country too.

There have been many blessings received.

More Solace members have been added to our numbers since we have been here, helping us by taking over some of the responsibilities.

The Lord always provides.

We now see beyond a shadow of a doubt that we needed this centre!

You may still be thinking that the Lord has asked quite a lot from me, especially to give up my home and business.

However, as I have explained, it was not too difficult for me because I did realise that all I had belonged to Him anyway and it was just a matter of using 'His' money in the way that He knew was for the best and in the way that would bring happiness.

I did say 'Lord, please make it right with my children,' after all they may well have been thinking that this money would one day have come to them.

I just hoped that they would understand and not think my actions a bit 'over the top'.

In fact one of my sons in law has recently confessed that, at the time, he had thought that I had 'lost the plot!'

However I had come to understand that when the Lord asks anything of us, He has complete control of the situation and He would take care of the consequences.

I am so happy to say that the Lord has indeed shown His great love and protection. This lovely son in law, who in the past he had been rather critical, is now actively seeking the Lord!

It is so wonderful to see his excitement in his new found faith and to hear him say

'I was blind then but now I can see!'

He has become a wonderful support for us at Star house and has become involved with my daughter and their four daughters with the much-needed redecoration of some of our rooms.

He is helping us too with advice on the computer programme we use, and is the support for all the co-ordinators from around the world

I am sure he will not mind my saying this, but all the family are truly amazed at this wonderful turnaround in his beliefs!

Praise the Lord! This, for my daughter and for me, is worth more than all the money in the world!

I would also like to share with you another way the Lord has shown His care.

After I had sold my house and paid off my mortgage, there was still some money left.

I wondered how the Lord wished me to use this money, and thought that perhaps I should buy a small flat to rent out, in order to receive an income.

I pursued this idea, but did not feel peaceful about it and indeed I just drew a blank for all my efforts. So I decided just to wait.

Not long after this, I became ill and it was then that I found that living in a community house was not so easy!

It can be difficult to feel relaxed when you are ill, and to have to stay in your bedroom.

It is not easy to wander round the house in a dressing gown or go to the kitchen to make some tea and toast when other people are around.

I must admit to having felt rather 'shut in'.

I prayed about this and felt that the Lord put it on my heart to buy a flat, not for an income, but for myself.

It made sense, because then I had a place that I could go to occasionally – to recharge my batteries, maybe to do some writing, and also to be with my family.

When I spoke to my Spiritual director later about this, he confirmed that this was indeed what I should do.

So together with some of my colleagues from the community, I started to look for a flat. I had thought it would be nice to have one with a sea view. I really love the sea!

(At the time of my 'surrender' I did have an apartment near the sea. It was rather beautiful and had a sea view from every room. When I left there, I thought that I would never again have such a place.)

We looked for several months to find a flat suitable to purchase, but without success.

So I began to think that perhaps it would be better to rent one.

A few weeks later, when I was visiting Westminster Cathedral I was greeted by one of the 'Mothers Prayers' members who lived by the sea, and in an area we had not yet visited.

When I told her that I was looking for a flat to rent, because I did not seem to be able to find a suitable one to buy, she invited me to come to see a flat she owned which she rented out occasionally. She lived in a really lovely area.

We decided to go there the next day and whilst we were there we decided to contact the estate agent not really expecting to find anything suitable. He told us of a flat for sale nearby which seemed to be exactly what we had been looking for and every room had a sea view!

The flat although it is much smaller than my former one, is exactly right for my circumstances now. Because it is smaller, the running costs are much cheaper. (I would not now be able to afford the running costs of the former apartment.) And I am much happier with this one.

(The neighbours too, are really lovely people and when I was ill recently they even brought me some food showing great love and concern.)

I really felt that the Lord had a hand in all of this; I could not have found a better place!

To make me feel even more blessed, I discovered that the price had been reduced by £5,000 only three days before.

This enabled me to furnish the flat, and have it redecorated.

Through all this I felt the Lord was showing me His love and concern and He has shown me this in smaller ways, too.

For example, I had left all my furnishings behind when I moved to 'Solace' (see page 57) and this certainly did not worry me at the time.

But when I was invited to visit my new friends, who had moved into my former home, I did find it quite sad to go into my old bathroom and use the towels I had chosen and had left behind – it does seem strange but this affected me more than seeing my old furniture again.

I had also left behind new bed linen of a rather pleasing design that I had just bought.

So when I moved to my new flat five years later, and went to visit a charity shop, you can imagine how surprised I was, to see the bed linen of the exact design as the one I had left behind in my old house. It was in absolutely new condition and at a fraction of the original price.

Yes, I really felt that the Lord was showing that He is interested even in the smallest detail of what is pleasing to us.

With each of these showings of His love, I become more aware of His wonderful closeness and concern for all that makes us happy, and I have come to know for certain that He will not be outdone in generosity!

5. *The Pentecost Celebrations*

Our 100% surrender will also include the way we work in our church or parish, whatever our role. And it is wise to ask the Lord to guide us in this.

When we feel the Lord asking us to do something, it is so easy to rush ahead without praying first to ask Him how He wants us to work.

I have found it a good practice to ask myself 'How much time have I spent on planning and how much time in prayer.' And 'have I got the balance right?'

In my former parish, I was for a time a member of the Deanery Pastoral Council; we were one of the seven parishes in the group.

Whilst I was serving on this council we arranged a celebration for Pentecost.

It was decided that an evening would be arranged to ask the Holy Spirit for a blessing on all people with special ministries and leaders of organisations within the parishes of the Deanery.

Each hour would be especially dedicated to a particular group. i.e. for those serving in a practical way by flower arranging, cleaning, serving on the altar, children's ministries, Eucharistic ministers and all family and prayer groups.

Because we were all very busy people, we did not have very much time to make plans, although we did decide to make sure we spent time in prayer in preparation for the event.

So we arranged that a member of the Deanery Pastoral Council from each church, would work with a priest from a neighbouring parish and they would decide how to spend an hour.

We did not know what the other leaders of the hours had arranged but trusted that it would all come together well.

We did not even know which hymns the other groups had arranged.

However, I am sure it was because we prayed and trusted that it was a very blessed evening.

More people came than we had thought would come and some, who had originally only anticipated staying for the hour for the blessing on their particular work, actually stayed the whole evening!

The programme was beautifully varied and none of the hymns were duplicated!

Some people even said they didn't want to go home and others that they would like to have such an evening every week.

The Lord really honoured our prayers.

6. Medical

The Lord will guide us – He is interested in all that we do.

I recently visited Russia. This time the visit was to last for five weeks and would include Belarus and Lithuania.

(I seem to have written quite considerably about Russia but I do visit many other countries too. It just seems these are the right examples for this book).

I had been experiencing a problem with my eye, although just before I left home it had seemed as if it was getting better.

However, after a few days in Moscow I realised that it was in fact getting worse.

The whole of my left eye had become blood red. My friends took me to the eye clinic and I was soon seen by the top eye specialist.

He diagnosed the condition but still felt that I should go into hospital for tests.

As I don't speak Russian, and did not know if I was covered financially by my insurance, I asked him if it would be harmful to fly back home. He assured me that it would be perfectly safe to do so.

I wasn't sure what to do. As we returned to our centre in Kaluga, I decided that I should pray first to ask the Lord what I should do because I had a suspicion that the evil one was trying to make me give up and go home.

Should I go home?…

I decided to stay the night and to pray. I thought that maybe the Lord would give me an answer through His Word as sometimes when I pray and then open the Bible, the answer is there for me in a very clear way. I thought that maybe in the passage I would read, there would be some direction.

But the next morning when I prayed, I said 'Lord who am I to demand an answer from you from the Bible. I know that you love me and you will show me what to do. I really would like to know what to do now.

I just want to do your Will and to be sure whether you want me to stay or go home.'

I did open the Bible and was completely overwhelmed when I saw the page I had opened at.

It was from Ecclesiasticus 34. v 9 The title? **Travelling!**

A much-travelled man knows many things,
And a man of great experience will talk sound sense.
Someone who has never had his trials knows little;
But the travelled man is master of every situation.
I have seen many things in my travels,
I have understood more than I can put into words.
I have often been in danger of death,
But have been spared, and this is why;
The spirit of those who fear the Lord can survive,

For their hope is in someone with power to save them.
No one who fears the Lord need ever hesitate,
Or ever be daunted, since the Lord is their hope.
Happy the soul of one who fears the Lord.
On whom does he rely? Who supports him?
The eyes of the Lord watch over those who love him,
He is their powerful protection and their strong
support
Their screen from the desert wind, their shelter from
the midday sun.
A guard against stumbling, an assurance against a
fall.
He revives the spirit and BRIGHTENS the EYES
He gives health, life and blessings.

I was very emotional as I said 'Lord, you are so near'
And, yes, I stayed!

This visit turned out to be one of many, many blessings. We had meetings with many mothers and with the new co-ordinators of 'Mothers Prayers' for Belarus, Lithuania and Poland.

We were even more greatly blessed, by a meeting with a lovely, gentle Archbishop from the Orthodox Church, who was a great encouragement to us. He welcomed us warmly and gave His blessing to 'Mothers Prayers'.

How close is our God!!

After a few days my eye had healed completely.

---

7. *Other peoples' experiences.*

Choices

We will always have to make some choices in our lives, because we have been given the dignity of having a free will, and we are able to choose how we accept every situation in our lives.

If we are surrendered to the Lord, He will guide us through all the difficult times and bring good out of the bad.

Often we are not able to control the circumstances in our lives, for example our health, our relationships and even our finances.

But we are able to choose how we *accept* these situations.

I know of two women who had been deserted by their husbands. They did not have the choice as to whether the husband left or not. However they did have the choice of how they reacted.

Obviously at first both were distraught, and had terrible feelings of anger, of rejection, of disbelief and later feelings of guilt thinking perhaps somehow it was their fault.

Later, however one of them, we will call her Mary, understood that to harbour all these negative feelings would only turn her into a bitter, angry and vindictive person. This would completely change her character

In giving all these feelings to the Lord, surrendering the situation, and asking for the grace to forgive, she was set free and became calm and able to start a new life in peace.

Joan, the other however, chose to remain angry, taking every opportunity to speak badly about her husband. Her greatest delight was to try to bring him into disrepute.

This not only affected her character, it also affected her health.

A *better way…*

Another example that comes to my mind is about my very close friend, Dorothy.

After she had retired from work, Dorothy discovered that she had cancer. During her illness she became very close to the Lord and we had the joy of being with her at her First Communion and Confirmation.

Her life was a real example of surrender. I never once heard her complain in all that time. During her illness she learnt calligraphy and painstakingly designed a picture for me with my favourite Bible text. It was so beautiful, but even more so, because of all the trouble she had taken to please me.

I had the privilege of being with her in the last hours of her life here.

We prayed together and the last words she whispered were, 'Thank you Jesus for being here with me'.

She then, very peacefully, went to meet her Maker.

In the same room in the hospice there was another cancer patient.

Sadly she did not have the same peace as Dorothy.

She complained often asking 'Why me?'

The visiting times for her relatives were quite an ordeal.

She died the day after Dorothy, and I could not help comparing their last hours here in this world and feeling so sad for that woman and for her family.

My mother's example…

I would like to mention my mother here too.

What a wonderful example she was to us and to all who met her.

Her life was not easy.

She was a convert to the Catholic faith in her teens. She married my father who was also a Catholic and looked forward to having a good Christian marriage.

They had us, six children, very quickly; in fact when the youngest was born the eldest was only eight.

It was at this time that my father left us. It is not for me to judge him, as my parents were quite different in their natures and backgrounds.

However as young children we prayed with our mother every night for my father, so that he would come back to his faith. We were reconciled to him in our adult life.

As I write this little booklet I am happy to say that our prayers were not wasted – in his latter years my father came back to his faith and only last week, he too went to meet his Maker, covered in prayer and after receiving the Sacraments.

The last six and a half years of my mother's life were spent in a hospital bed.

She had a massive heart attack and a stroke. She was unable to move and had to be turned every two hours. She was also unable to feed herself and could not even reach for a cup of water. Her speech too, was affected and it was only with great difficulty and patience that she managed to make herself understood.

It was often, only by going through the alphabet with her, saying each letter and then waiting to know if this was the first letter of the word she was trying to say, and then continuing like this, until a whole word was formed that we managed to communicate at all.

However her mind seemed to be unaffected.

She knew everything that was going on and spent much of her time praying.

She was a wonderful example of surrender, she was much loved by the nurses and they all said that there was something different about her room. I am sure it was all the prayers that were said there.

We were called to her bedside many times, being told that she was on the point of dying. We would sit and pray for her.

Often the next day, she would be propped up in bed being fed her breakfast as usual.

The doctors and staff said 'Your mother will go when the good Lord wants her'. She defied all medical expectations.

Even those who did not have a relationship with God knew there was something special going on!

Perhaps you may think that it would have been better for her to have died in those early years of her illness. All I can say is that during this time *we* grew spiritually and were very blessed during the constant visiting, and others were too.

We shared our stories with her – she was interested in everything.

She knew all about 'Mothers Prayers' and I am sure this brought her great comfort.

Our relationship with her deepened too, as we spent time in prayer with her.

She was still guiding us even from her bed.

We used to pray with other patients too and often organised little prayer meetings for them.

My mother never did seem to realise how ill she was and I am sure by this that the Lord kept her from suffering too much!

She is a wonderful example of how we can be used by the Lord, whatever our circumstances!

How valuable to the world are the prayers of the elderly!

If only we would acknowledge this more often, and encourage them by telling them how they are able to help to change the lives of others by their prayers.

I would like to share with you an illustration of 'choice' that I feel the Lord gave to me through a 'picture' during prayer.

It was of a train, that was stationary in a tunnel as it had broken down..

Inside one carriage were two men who were grumbling and getting very agitated, as they paced up and down looking at their watches.

As time went by they became more and more angry.

In another carriage there was a man who, realising there was a problem, sat down and put his feet up. The guard then came in and offered him a cup of tea. All was calm.

When the train started again and came out of the tunnel, I noticed that the tunnel was actually made of crystal.

What I felt the Lord saying through this was, that we all at some stage go into a dark place, like a tunnel, it might be a long or a short one, and we might not know when we will come out again.

However, we do have a choice; we can either get angry, blame others or even God,

or we can sit back and let the Lord (just like the guard), minister to us as we wait to come out again into the sunshine.

The train did not start again any more quickly through all the agitation of those two men and the result was that they left in a very angry frame of mind.

I felt the Lord was saying that even in the darkest tunnel if you invite him in there with you it will become a very precious place.

(Remember the tunnel was made of crystal)

8. *General.*

I do believe that the gift of surrender is for everyone, and I am sure that the Lord is calling us all to come closer to Him through this.

It is by our response and willingness to allow Him to guide us, that we will find new life.

Perhaps you may be thinking that this is all right for you Veronica: you have been given a special grace.

God has no favourites. I am sure He wants us all to live in this way and if He can use someone like me and bless me so much, He will surely do the same for you – all He needs is your 'YES'.

You may ask 'What then, can I expect to happen through surrender?'

I believe that for most people there will not be any immediate change in their lifestyle, or seemingly none, (they are usually gradual). The Lord alone knows your needs and it is always His perfect timing.

Sometimes we change without really noticing it, until one day we realise that we have lost the taste for former things, even those that before were very important to us.

You must have no fear and remember He is a God of love. He knows how much you can cope with.

He will take you by the hand and lead you step by step to your real place.

He will bring the right people to you who will help you.

If you are married, He will help you to be a better spouse, more loving and contented. He will guide you in your work, in your private life, in your relationships with others.

If you have a vocation to the priesthood or religious life he will lead you in your ministry giving you a new and deeper peace.

Whatever your calling, he will confirm it, change it or deepen it, whatever is necessary.

He will help you to grow in Him and in love for others and so enjoy the blessing of being truly human and truly alive.

He will use you for His purposes to help others.

It will be unnecessary to keep worrying and asking what to do or what will happen.

You will just need to keep praying and carry on with your life.

He will give you little reassurances that He is there and ALL is well.

He will speak to you in your innermost being, perhaps through a thought, an image in your imagination, through a verse of Scripture, through other people and even by words that come to your mind, which you know are not your own words.

You will get to know His voice.

If you have surrendered your life to Him 100%, you need not be worried that you have heard correctly – just ask Him 'Lord if this is from you please make it so clear that I will have no doubts, please protect me from any thoughts that do not come from you, please block anything that is not of your Holy Will'

If you are still not sure then wait until it does become clear. He will not let you go astray; and if you sincerely want only to do His Will and you were to miss something important, He will remind you.

'Be still and know that I am God' Psalm 46.

The change however may be quite dramatic.

If we have been going in the wrong direction the change may well be quite dramatic.

It was so for me, some of the changes were painful, but I can tell you that I have never been so happy in my life, as I am now.

It is such a comfort to know that, because I have surrendered my life into His care, He is in charge of every situation and so all is well. Even the seemingly bad things that may happen – can turn out to be a blessing and these are often the very means of our growth.

What more could one wish for?

Does this mean that we cease to have any sad feelings, that we will always feel happy? – No, of course not. In fact the closer we come to the Lord, the more sensitive we become and more aware of the pain in the world.

But we soon learn that the more quickly we surrender our feelings of pain and our hurts to Him, the sooner our peace is restored again.

I have often said 'Lord, I don't like this situation too much, it's painful. But because I have asked You to be in charge of my life, I accept it and ask you to use this pain as a prayer for......'

My peace is quickly restored and I feel the joy of His closeness.

I have often found later, that the very thing that was so painful was necessary for my progress towards Him and I thank Him for His goodness.

But it is important and necessary to renew our act of surrender frequently; even every day, as the evil one will always be there to try to lead us astray.

It is also important to remind ourselves that we are nothing without Him. In feeling blessed through our surrender it could be so easy to become self-righteous, as though we had everything and nothing could touch us.

Yes, life will always have some pain and trials, but we will never lose our Peace if we remain focused on His Will. And as I have experienced it is quite possible to actually feel *JOY* amongst the pain, in the knowledge that all is well because everything is in His Hands.

Other consequences:

I hope that through these pages so far I have been able to show you how the Lord will lead us step by step through our surrender in all situations.

If I were asked what I feel are the results of my 'surrender' to the Will of God, I would say **FREEDOM!**

Freedom from fear and worry:-

❖ of the future

❖ of change

❖ of making decisions

❖ of what other people think

I have found that it is possible to live in joy and peace – whatever the circumstances, and to know that the plans of the Beloved will unfold.

Also that all striving and uncertainties will cease if we become responding people instead of wanting to be initiators, just happy to be led with no need or wish to be in control.

It has also meant not having to wear masks.

Since my surrender the words of Scripture have become so alive to me and speak deeply to my heart now in a new way.

I am much more appreciative of the wonderful gift of the Holy Eucharist and the importance for me of daily Mass.

It has not meant immunity from pain but that it is possible to be joyful in spite of it knowing that all is in the Will of the Lord and He will bring good out of every circumstance.

To me it is the Pearl of Great Price!

How safe it is to rely on the Lord's leadings when we come to understand that He, who loves much, is now in charge of our lives.

I do want to stress that these have been my personal experiences and may not be the same way that the Lord will lead you. For example when preparing for a meeting He may wish you to make notes; the important thing is to be led by Him.

He will guide each one of us in the way that is right for our personality, circumstances and for the plans He has for each one of us.

'I alone know the plans I have for you, plans to bring you prosperity and not disaster, plans to bring about the future you hope for.'

Jeremiah 29 v 11

All He is waiting for is our 'YES'.

I am so sure that surrender is a gift that the Lord wishes us all to accept.

Section 3: How to surrender and how God's guidance comes

1. Love God

It has been suggested that I repeat one of the pages from the beginning of this book.

Maybe you are wondering 'What must I do to surrender and what will it mean to my life?' Or perhaps you feel the cost may prove to be too high.

I do understand that it may seem difficult, as it is contrary to our usual way of thinking. We usually feel we must strive to 'be in control' and it is our responsibility to find all the solutions to our problems.

And so it may be difficult for you to even consider 'surrender' as something to be sought after.

One of the reasons you may be worried, is that you may think that the Lord will want you to be poor and expect you to give everything away, in the same way He asked the rich young man in the Bible.

But only He knows the special plan He has for you, the one that will make you happy and feel fulfilled. If it is for you to work and be amongst the poor, you will never be truly happy if you try to be in any other place.

His plan for you may be to be amongst the rich and if so that is where you will find happiness.

It is more likely that He will wish you to remain just where you are now and by the way you live, be a witness of

---

His love and protection, to your friends, neighbours and people at work.

It is not about being poor or wealthy; it is about being where the Lord wants you to be – to have no agenda of your own, except to do His Will.

And remember that if we do surrender our lives to Him, this includes our financial situation but it also means He will look after our overdrafts too.

We are only the managers of His money. There is great freedom in this.

In the past, I have watched the worried expressions of some people when I have touched on the subject of total surrender. But after I have had the following conversation with them, their expression has usually changed.

I ask them 'are you married?' and when they reply 'yes',

I continue; 'when you were standing at the altar on your wedding day, did you not surrender your life to your spouse?

Did you not say, 'for better for worse, for richer for poorer, in sickness and in health, till death do us part' and isn't this 'surrender'?

Were you not willing to go wherever was necessary to support them and to stay with them forever whatever the circumstances?

In other words you both surrendered your lives to each other.

And you did this I am sure because you loved your spouse, and you knew that you were loved too.'

I do wonder why so many people are worried about making similar promises to their Lord and God – He, who can never let them down, who loves them passionately and wishes only for their good!

You may even be thinking I am not good enough; there is too much sin in my life.

The Lord himself said 'I have come to call not the upright but sinners to repentance.'

He knows our hearts and if we sincerely want to come closer to Him, He will take us by the hand and lead us. He waits longingly for our return to Him.

2. Know God.

After I had written the first draft of this book, I took it to my Spiritual director who suggested to me that I should also include some guidance on how to surrender.

This gave me a bit of a problem; because to me all that was necessary was that we should kneel down and bare our soul to the Father telling Him of our desire to live life His way! To ask Him to change us so that we would live our life as the person He had created us to be.

After reflecting on this, I realised that it is almost impossible to surrender to anyone unless we know, love and trust them. (as in Marriage).

For how can we surrender our will to someone we don't really know and love?

We need to know the Lord personally, not just know about Him.

How do we do this?

❖ If we do not really understand the great love the Lord has for us we should pray and ask the Holy Spirit to reveal this to us. He will help us come to know of the great unconditional love the Father has for each one of us, and the love of Jesus, His Son.

❖ We learn about this love in the Scriptures as we see all the examples throughout the ages that are recorded there. These are just as relevant for us today, and the Lord will speak to our hearts through His Word.

❖ We need to experience His presence in our daily lives, so it is good to develop a habit of chatting frequently to the Lord about every day matters, always asking for guidance and spending time listening to Him.

❖ We need to accept that we are lovable, even though we know we have failed, for He loves each one of us passionately.

3. Practical steps.

We prepare our hearts by:

- ❖ acknowledging our need of Him.

- ❖ repenting of our sins before Him.

- ❖ forgiving those who have harmed us.

- ❖ trying to be faithful in little things.

- ❖ spending time in Praising Him.

- ❖ telling Him that we are willing to be changed.

- ❖ asking Him to give us a teachable spirit, and a listening open heart.

He asks us to come as children totally trusting in His fatherly love.

'Surrender' means just that – we go to our Heavenly Father with all our needs having no ambition, except to do His Will. He will be ambitious for us – He knows what will make us happy!

*This is such a hurting world and many people seem
to have lost their way, we can either join them in
their despair and think that all is lost,
Or we can say 'Maranatha'*

*Come Lord Jesus,
I want you 100% in my life
to be your hands and your feet
so that You can work through me*

---

to make a difference to this world.
I want to help others to come to You
to be filled with your Holy Spirit
so that when You come again,
many people will be waiting.

Section 4: Scripture and Prayer.

Words of Love from Jesus to you!

I would call you and call you;
I call you to come to me;
I want you to experience my Spirit as a fountain welling up
in your heart. (Jn 7:37–39)

*The Way you must go – it is **myself**;*
*The Truth you need – it is **myself**;*
I am the Life you must live – everlasting Life in the Father.(Jn 14:6)

The food you need to live forever – living substance. (Jn 6:51)

*The only light the world needs –**all** the light it needs, is **myself**.*

(Jn 9:5)

To you, I will always be as a shepherd who loves his sheep
*And is ready to die for any one of them – **For you**.*
(Jn 10)

The Joy of Surrender unto Him!

The life which will be in you when you rise from
*the dead – it is **I**. (Jn 11:25)*
The Spirit whom I give you, He is a tender loving
friend to you,
And cannot be anything else. (Jn 14:26, 15:26)
*The Life you need is Light, and it is in **me**. (Jn 1:4)*

I give you power to be child of my Father, of God
himself. (Jn 1:12)
I am full of all you need – and I give it to you.
(Jn 1:16)
Believe in me and you will live forever. (Jn 3:15)
I will slake your thirst, and the water will be in you
like a spring – forever. (Jn 4:14)

*My father is **your** dear and loving Father too.*
(Mt 6:9)
You may be selfish and heartless, but my Father will
be kind (Lk 6:35)

I will raise you up to be with me when the time
comes. (Jn 6:44)
You have eaten my Flesh and drunk my Blood
(Jn 6:55)
You are now living in me and I in you.
(Jn 6 55–57)

I give Life to whomsoever I wish to; and I give it to you (Jn 5:21)
Come with me! (Mt 4:19)

No one will ever snatch you away from me.
(Jn 10:28)

Never be frightened! (Lk 12:32)

You're weighed down? Come to me! (Mt 11:28)

Yes, Jesus longs for us to come to Him – He wants to heal our broken hearts, He wants to lead us on the path to holiness and happiness!

I hope that some of the suggested readings from Scripture and the following prayers will help you to come to know, in a deeper way, the power and supply of our God and of His great love for you, personally.

It may help that when you read the suggested passages from Scriptures, you imagine that you are in the scene and let the words speak to you as if they had been written especially for you.

You may like to use the prayers suggested or to say your own prayers – just simple words from your heart to His.

Read… St Paul's letter to Ephesians 1 v 17–20

May the God of our Lord Jesus Christ, the Father of Glory, give you a spirit of Wisdom, and perception of what is revealed, to bring you to a full knowledge of Him. May He enlighten the eyes of your mind so that you can see what hope his call holds for you, how rich is the glory of the heritage he offers among his holy people and how extraordinarily great is the power that he has exercised for us believers; this accords with the strength of his power.

Pray…

Dear Holy Spirit,
I come to you to ask for your help and guidance.
You already know what is in my heart -
I really want to experience the Love the Father has for me.
It is such an awesome thought
that He should love *me* personally!
I want to **know** Jesus too, not just about Him
Help me to seek and discover God's will for my life
And please give me a teachable spirit,
So that I will be open to accept any changes that need to be made in order that I may live completely within the Father's Will.

Amen

The Joy of Surrender unto Him!

Read… Jeremiah 31 v 3. Luke 15 v 11–32. Psalm 32.

Pray…

Dear Father in Heaven,
I want to see you as my loving father,
Like the one who welcomed back
The prodigal son with open arms.
Please forgive me, for the times
I have wandered away from you
And thank you that you still love me in spite of this
Please forgive me for any lack of trust in your mercy.
Let me be truly free from all the guilt of the past
And rest in the knowledge that your love and forgiveness
Is total.
And please give me the grace to forgive all those who
have hurt me.
Amen.

Read... Genesis 1 v 1 Genesis 2 v 4. Genesis 18
v 13–14
John 3 v 16. Ps 8.

Pray.....

Dear Lord,
You are Almighty God
And nothing is too difficult for you
You are all powerful, the creator of all.
You spoke and it came to be.
You have a wonderful plan for each one of us.
Yes, I acknowledge that nothing is too difficult for you.
You hold the whole world in your hands.
Help me always to remember that you have power
Over everything and every situation.
Thank you that you gave us your only Son, Jesus,
So that we would have eternal life.
Please help me to appreciate this great act of love.
Amen

Read... Exodus 16 v 4 Luke 9 v 10–17 Matthew 6 v 25–34

Pray...

Thank you dear Lord,
For your constant provision.
You know our needs
Even before we know them ourselves.
Please give us the grace
To trust you
And to rely on you for everything
Amen

———————————————

Read... Isaiah 40 v 11 Luke 15 v 4–7

Pray...

Dear Jesus,
Thank you that you are the Good Shepherd.
And you gave your life for me.
I am one of your sheep that was lost
Thank you for finding me
And bringing me back to the fold.
Amen

Read... Luke 23 v 39–43.

Pray...

Dear Jesus
Thank you that you are an ever-loving God,
And that you never reject us
You show us that you are always willing to forgive us
No matter what we have done.
Just as you forgave the repentant thief
Who died next to you on the cross
Thank you that it is never too late
To ask for your forgiveness
Amen..

Read... Psalm 139

Pray...

Dear Jesus
Please help me always to be conscious of your presence
And to know that you are interested
In **everything** I do.
Whether I am driving the car, or at my work place
Cleaning the house or preparing meals,
Remind me to speak to you often and to share my thoughts
(The good and the bad) with you.
You are my dearest and closest friend.
Amen.

———————————————

Read... Philippians 4 v 6,7 Isaiah 43 v 1–5 1 John 4 v 18. Luke 11 v 9–13.

Pray...

Dear Lord
When I am anxious and fearful
And find it difficult to trust completely in you,
Please help me to focus on your promises
And not on my own abilities

In the past I have often felt that *I* must be in control.
So I know it may be difficult to leave everything with you.
Please give me this grace to 'let go'
And bring my worries and concerns to you,
Confidently knowing that
You have everything in your hands.
And that in your perfect time and in your perfect way
My prayers will be answered.
Please give me the grace of perseverance.
Amen.

————————————————

Read… Luke 1 v 38 Matthew 9 v 9 Matthew 6 v 19-21

Pray…

Dear Lord,
Please let me say without hesitation 'Your will be done'
As Mary did, when the angel brought your message to her.
Help me to be unafraid of the consequences of my 'Yes'.
Please give me the grace
Of joyful obedience.
Take away any fear of the future
So that I may go forward unafraid
In the knowledge that you love me
And wish only good things for me.
Amen.

Dear Lord,
When I hear your voice
Or feel you asking something of me
Please help me to respond like Matthew
Whose life you changed from a despised tax collector
To an Evangelist!
Thank you that you will guide me
And show me your ways
Through your Holy Spirit
Amen.

––––––––––––––––––––

Read... Psalm 91

Pray...

Dear Lord,
Please make me more aware of how safe it is
To place my life, and my future in your hands.
You are my loving father and almighty God!
Thank you for your great love for me.
Amen.

Prayer of Surrender.

Dear Father,
When I say 'Thy Will be done on earth as it is in Heaven',
Please let me add from the bottom of my heart,
'Thy Will be done in my life too'.
Father I wish to consecrate myself to you right now.
I know I need to change, but
I ask *You* to help me to change.
I desire to be the person you created me to be.
I wish to live in accordance with your Holy Will.
And to fulfil the special plan you have for my life.
Please give me the grace and the joy of Surrender.
Amen.

We pray that we may say the words
St Paul wrote in his *letter to the Philippians 3 v 7-14*

I believe that nothing can happen that will outweigh the supreme advantage of knowing Christ Jesus my Lord. For Him I have accepted the loss of everything, and I look on everything as so much rubbish if only I can have Christ and be given a place in Him.

I am no longer trying for perfection by my own efforts, the perfection that comes from the Law, but I want only the perfection that comes through faith in Christ, and is from God based on faith.

All I want is to know Christ and the power of His resurrection and to share in His sufferings by reproducing the pattern of His death.

That is the way I can hope to take my place in the resurrection of the dead.

Not that I have become perfect yet; I have not yet won, but I am still running, trying to capture the prize for which Christ Jesus captured me.

I can assure you, my brothers, I am far from thinking that I have already won. All I can say is that I forget the past and strain for what is still to come; I am racing for the finish, for the prize to which God call us upwards to receive in Christ Jesus.

In conclusion: Is all this safe?

Yes, I repeat from the introduction: much of what Veronica says about "Surrender" has classic parallels. De Caussade speaks of Abandonment to Divine Providence, Brother Lawrence of the Practice of the Presence of God.

It seems one can identify what she speaks of in their words. And with her too there are arresting consequences from the Act of Surrender, in the way of finding God's Will.

Now most would say there are three areas where God's Will is found.

First, by the practical dictation of it in the circumstances He wills or allows in the present moment.

Secondly, in his stated commands.

Thirdly, and more subtly, He can make His "unknown" Will clearer to us by moving our spirit.

The third area is that of "discernment of spirits", and is normally, in Ignatian spirituality, a matter of testing and weighing "consolation and desolation".

Always it presupposes a high degree of freedom: unless one is free to do or un-do whatever God may ask, and unless one really wants to know, it is unlikely He will bother to tell us. This freedom, the achievement of it, the cost and the exercise of it, Veronica shows very clearly.

In practice God can irrupt into someone's life and makes His will blindingly clear, as with St. Paul. But more probably God will work more gently by nudges, winks, nods, head shake; by consolation or desolation, by movement of the spirit.

John Edwards S.J.